# TESTIMONIALS

We seemed to have been friends forever, so when we were greeted with the fabulous news that Jim and Karin Keays were expecting a new addition to their wonderful family, we were overjoyed. So, it would be Jim, Karin, Holly and Bonnie. And of course the new child (William), who would be a boy – almost too perfect for words.

That perfect scenario unfortunately took a dramatic turn when, on what was supposed to be the most joyous day of all, tragedy struck.

Losing a child has to be one of the greatest tragedies to be inflicted upon anyone.

You can sympathise and offer as much of yourself as you can – but you can never really descend to the depths of sorrow that the family is suffering.

Karin's book gives us glimmers and insights into that lonely, and solely individual, suffering as each parent is trying to deal with their own pain separately. Holly and Bonnie had to carry their own burdens as well. Four people, together but ironically separated by their own sufferings.

Karin's story is deeply personal, and for her to let us all in, and take us through this incredibly painful journey, is a vulnerability that many people could not share. It is a journey worth taking with her – at times very painful, with a helplessness attached – however, her spirit, along with her enduring positive vision for her future, is inspiring. And with her every step of the way is William, who resides in her heart and soul, for he is forever remembered.

- Russell Morris AM

I remember sitting on our back stairs one evening with Jim and Glenn telling stories, some of which may have had an element of truth, and I couldn't help thinking how much I loved seeing Jim and Karin together. They were so happy and complemented each other in EVERY way, and of course were such a gorgeous looking couple.

Jim was heavily featured on my bedroom wall when I was a teenager and the Masters Apprentices records were on high rotation on my record player. How I ended up married to the bass player for 40 years is another story. How Karin had never heard the song 'Because I Love You' when she met Jim just goes to show how much younger than me Karin is!

When Karin told me she was writing a book I naturally assumed it would be about the life she shared with Jim Keays, and the roller coaster ride that is the world of rock and roll.

When I was able to read the manuscript, nothing prepared me for the story of Billy Keays.

This is a story of a mother's love, her heartache and quest for the truth.

With no agenda other than to find out what happened to her son Karin proceeded to question the system and those we put our trust in.

I could only imagine Karin's pain and yet she was able to continue, not only to breathe, but to function as a wife and mother while fighting the legal system and questioning the medical fraternity.

It is an incredulous story... one I urge you to read.

To date, and after so many years, Karin has affected real change, and I couldn't be more proud of her for telling this story.

As a mother and grandmother whose children and grandchildren will benefit from these changes, I can only thank her and Billy from the bottom of my heart.

- Gaynor Wheatley

It is right that we remember Jim Keays as the singer with the Master's Apprentices. It is easy to recall him as the Boy from the Stars. Like the band he so famously fronted across those febrile years when music was upended again and again, he was obsessed with the blues, adopted and helped reshape psychedelic pop, before writing some hard rock classics and diving into long vinyl progressive adventures.

It was a restlessly eclectic journey in music. He lived and loved life to the full.

Jim's private life was also a battle for heroes. Here, his wife Karin Keays details the patchwork quilt that was his heritage and how he respected that while proving his love for his own family as he contested the fates time and again.

- Alan Howe, The Australian.

# IT'S BECAUSE I LOVE YOU

### Karin Keays

Contempo Publishing

*For the Love of*
*William*

652 Hogans Rd North Tumbulgum NSW 2490.
www.contempopublishing.com
Copyright © Karin Keays 2024.

All rights reserved. No part of this book may be reproduced or transmitted by any person or entity, including internet search engines or retailers (including, but not limited to, Google and Amazon), in any form or by any means, electronic or mechanical, including photocopying (except under the statutory exceptions provisions of the Australian Copyright Act 1968), recording, scanning or by any information storage and retrieval system without the prior written permission of Contempo Publishing.

The moral rights of the author have been asserted.

A catalogue entry for this book is available from the National Library of Australia.

ISBN (Paperback):        978-0-6458077-9-0

Cover design by Rubi Creations Digital.
Proofreading by Sandra Balyoni.
Internal design by Contempo Publishing.

Printed and distributed internationally by Ingram Spark.
First published in 2024 by Contempo Publishing.

# Foreword

## By Sahara Herald
### *Tour Director, Frontier Touring*

The ties that bind two people together can be many and varied, reaching far beyond the traditional scope of marriage and bloodlines.

Jim Keays was Brad's (my husband's) friend, his mentor to some extent, both great admirers of each other's music, creativity, style and sharing a passion for cultural minutiae. I'd met Jim's wife Karin in passing at Brad's and my wedding, a rock'n'roll affair on Valentine's Day 1999, a rumbunctious celebration with a motley crew of friends and family. It was a brief encounter amongst the giddy blur of faces and well-wishers, but I was struck by Karin's beauty and poise amongst the rowdy revellers.

Thus, I was somewhat puzzled to receive an envelope out of the blue in the mail some years later, with Karin's name as the sender on the reverse. Inside was a beautiful card featuring some of Jim's unique artwork on the front, a drawing of Westminster Abbey. Intrigued, I opened it to read a tale all too familiar to me, of the heart-wrenching loss of their darling son William just hours after his traumatic birth. The pain of losing my own daughter Maddie a few years earlier stung afresh, a wound that had never quite healed, now once again open and weeping.

It's a pain you don't want to share in, you don't want anyone else to be afflicted by, a torturous blackhole of anguish and despair. Yet there was a strange sense of relief to know that maybe my own experience might in turn help someone else through their darkest hour, that we needn't walk the path alone. And so began a friendship ignited initially by grief but sustained on trust and camaraderie, and sometimes shared anger and shame and guilt but always honest, vulnerable and indelible in its foundation.

Over the past many years we supported each other through other losses, my divorce and Jim's sad passing. Through illnesses and disease, and recovery and remission. Through career challenges and triumphs. And all the while our beloved daughters Holly, Bonnie and Drew were finding their own paths – we proudly let them grow and flourish and occasionally flounder but ever watching with the cautious eyes only the mothers of the departed can possess.

Loss and grief can strangely intertwine with joy and celebration, twisting, turning, blurring across time and generations. True resilience is born of experience, as is lasting camaraderie. Karin, my love, I'm so very grateful that our stories are bound and we get to traverse life's strange journey together.

# Introduction

Once upon a time, I had a Friday tradition. I would walk up to the local shops in High Street and collect the latest copy of my favourite magazine.

Back at home, I'd make a nice cup of Irish Breakfast tea in my favourite Spode Blue Italian teacup. If it was a nice day, I'd take it out on the verandah, but usually I would settle in the lounge room with my tea and ten-weeks-behind edition of the English *Country Life*!

I still love that magazine. It is a well-written and beautifully photographed journal of country life in Britain and the issues affecting country people.

Open the front cover, and you will find the property section. Jim and I used to love drooling over the houses for sale.

We liked to pick out our favourites – it might be the 'important 16th century *piano nobile* on the Grand Canal that was the Venetian residence of Lord Byron, price on application.' Or, our more modest choice that week, a thatched cottage in Dorset with 'wonderful gardens including wildflower meadows, and a stretch of the River Wriggle with woodland walks.'

Before all that, though, I would invariably open *Country Life* to the back page first, to read *Spectator* by Carla Carlisle.

Carla Carlisle was born in America, a true Southern woman. She lived the lifestyle of a writer in Paris before marrying an English nobleman and becoming Lady Carlisle.

I have always admired Carla's writing style, her wit and her courage in sharing her sense of humour and opinions with anyone who cared to read them.

During our first trip to England in 1994, I began reading *Country Life*. I also began writing freelance travel articles, which, to my delight, were published in newspapers around Australia. It was after reading Carla's weekly column that I was inspired to have a go at submitting them for publication.

Then, in 1999, I read that the next week's edition would be the final *Spectator*. I waited and waited but that copy of *Country Life* never made it to Australia. For years after, I would feel a flash of annoyance each time I opened the back page and wondered what Carla wrote in her final column.

One day, many months after William's death, I opened *Country Life* to find Carla Carlisle's face smiling out at me. *Spectator* was back!

I read of tea and crafts in the barn café at Wyken, their Suffolk estate, and of coffee amongst the peacocks in the garden and felt as if I had visited with an old friend. I felt a vague shadow of joy, an emotion that I had resigned myself to never feeling again, but I still wanted to know what she had written in her final column!

So, I wrote to ask, not really expecting a reply.

Time rolled on, then, one day I received a beautiful hardcover book in the mail along with a card and hand-written note from Carla Carlisle!

*South Facing Slope* by Carla Carlisle is usually to be found on the top of the pile of books on my bedside table. It inspired me to begin collating my own collection of writings and research beginning from the birth of our son, William, and which form the basis of this book.

From my ritual Friday afternoon tea spent reading *Country Life*, I found inspiration.

Inspired by Carla's eloquence, I remembered that I too can write and found a way to share with others the knowledge that I now have – knowledge that I wish I had before William was born.

This book is for everyone, and not only for fans of my husband's music and music in general. It is for parents, grandparents and parents-to-be, their families and friends. It is for lovers and lovers of romance. It is for anyone who has ever wondered what it's like being the wife and partner of a rock legend. It is for bereaved parents, for the families and friends of the bereaved and for anyone who has experienced an adverse medical event in their family. Most importantly, it is for young women. The words in this book were written for my daughters, for their friends and for all young women. This true love story holds knowledge and experience that I wish had been shared with me as a young woman.

By the time you read this, you can be sure that a book from the first print run has been signed and sent to a country estate in Suffolk. I like to think – I hope – that when she receives it, Carla Carlisle will be justifiably proud.

# IT'S BECAUSE
# I LOVE YOU

**A Real-Life Rock'n'Roll Love Story**

# Prologue

### The English Lake District
### September 2013

There are places on this Earth where I have felt so close to Heaven that I could almost touch it, hear it, see it.

The English Lake District, one early autumn day, is one of those places. High on a fell (the Lakeland word for hill) near the summit. There were many trees, mainly Mountain Ash, which were laden with red berries and black birds. It was beneath one of those trees that I sat this particular autumn day. Before me lay a breathtaking panorama of lake, forest, distant fells and sky. I have never been able to behold such beauty without being awestruck.

The Lake District is famous for its natural beauty for good reason. The constant play of light on lakes, land and sky means that a single vista can change before your eyes countless times. Clouds form and reform, changing the sky and landscape. Sometimes patches of blue allow golden sunrays to spotlight distant hillsides and fields for a handful of moments before turning the steely water of the lake to a glittering ribbon, then moving on again. This is the land that inspired Poet Laureate, William

Wordsworth. It is the place where Beatrix Potter lived, wrote and illustrated her much-loved stories of Peter Rabbit, Samuel Whiskers and Mrs. Tiggy-Winkle. To this day, it is a honey-pot for artists along with tourists and outdoors types.

An unfamiliar peace settled deep in my heart, and I lay back on soft grass, letting Mother Earth enfold me in her loving energy. Through the tangled branches overhead, the sky was a soft grey. Just inches from the crown of my head lay a small posy of flowers and holly leaves, handpicked from the garden of my adored late father-in-law, Sam.

Two years ago, I carried Sam's ashes here to this same place and sprinkled them beneath the tree where the ground would not be walked on. With me was my dear friend, Mick, a retired military man, a man of loyalty and integrity. We followed the path less trodden up the hill and I held the container of ashes, grey plastic in a red velvet drawstring pouch, close to my chest.

As we walked, my arms began to ache, my back and shoulders tightening. More than once, Mick offered to take a turn carrying Sam, but I demurred. This was the last thing I could do for a good man who loved me and who I loved in return.

Two years ago, it had been summer, but the day had been overcast then, too. I looked up at the sky through the leaves, my thoughts touching lightly on the myriad changes in my life over those two years; then, as thoughts do, slipped back in time to one September day many years earlier…

## Chapter One

# To Your Heart Be True

*"My best friend is the one who brings out the best in me."*
*~ Henry Ford*

When I first met Jim in 1988, I was 23 years old and had arrived in Melbourne only hours earlier. I had just completed a solo road trip from the Gold Coast to stay with my friend, Snezana, another fun-loving Sagittarian. We had been instant friends from the moment we met five years earlier when we worked around the corner from each other in the city. Snezana managed a boutique in Flinders Street, and I went in one day on my lunch break. The most exotic creature was standing at the counter, speaking on the phone in a husky contralto. Fascinated, I sidled between the racks of clothes, pretending to browse whilst stealing furtive glances at the girl who looked like an early eighties reincarnation of Cleopatra! Sleek black hair cut in a long, geometric bob, her fringe had a huge streak of hot pink to one side, her eyeliner was straight off an ancient Egyptian fresco and her layered dress was strategically torn and swathed in studded belts. Then she hung up the phone, asked me if I'd like a glass of champagne and we've never looked back. That was in the early eighties and I had since moved back to my hometown of the Gold Coast. I'd missed my family but once back there, I also missed my friends in Melbourne and the more sophisticated lifestyle that it offered.

In 1987, I remember calling my parents into the lounge room to watch Snezana on the TV, dancing as a gogo girl on *Hey Hey It's Saturday*. I didn't know the band or the song and took little notice of them. It would be years after Jim died before I saw that clip again and the penny dropped. The band was Masters Apprentices and the guy in the middle was my future husband. Snezana, who would introduce me to that man a year later, was dancing in a cage beside him, resplendent in faux fur.

*

In 1988, I was nursing a broken heart and, as best friends do, Snezana came up with a plan. Move back to Melbourne so we could be together, work really hard for three months and save enough money to live our dream and travel the world. Snezana had contacts in Japan and I had studied Japanese at school so that was to be our first stop. At the time, I worked as manager of a Gold Coast store for a national fashion retail chain so I asked the question and was told there would be a position waiting for me in a city store in Melbourne if I wanted it!

In true Sagittarian fashion, everything was working out in our favour. All I needed was a place to live, a short-term rental for three months. My only prerequisite was a garage for my car, a brand new Ford Laser in Monza Red. Snezana is a can-do powerhouse sort of girl, always has been, and she had been on the lookout for me.

A couple of weeks before I was due to leave the Gold Coast, she called to say she had the perfect place for me – a huge house owned by a sixties rock star. His name was Jim Keays, from a band called Masters Apprentices.

"I've never heard of them," I said. Privately, I was thinking she must have been exaggerating about the rock star part. I love music and was pretty certain I knew of all the big Australian bands.

"Masters Apprentices?" Snezana could not believe it. "How come you've never heard of them? They were huge!"

"Maybe… tell me one of their songs. How does it go?"

"Their biggest one is 'Because I Love You' and it's on the new Lee Jeans commercial!" she said.

She started singing to me down the line, "Do what you wanna do, be what you wanna be, yeah…" I could tell she expected me to realise I knew it but I hadn't seen the commercial or heard the song.

"I don't know it, sorry. Just tell me, does this place have a garage?" The song sounded very hippie to me, and I wasn't into sixties music.

Snezana's sound of frustration was hilarious.

"YES! It has a DOUBLE garage for your precious car so you can pick your spot!" Sounding mystified and incredulous, she mused, "I can't believe you don't know that song!"

"Oh well, I'm going to be there for three months so I'm sure I'll get to know it."

A few days later, Snezana called to say she had arranged for me to meet Jim and see the house on the day I arrived.

"Can you get here any earlier? They are filming the clip for their new single and looking for a girl with long, dark hair just like you," she said, "You would be perfect!"

It sounded very exciting and tempting but I had given my notice at work and couldn't let my employer down, especially as they had been so good about finding a job for me in their Melbourne store.

Ironically, it was on the night before I met Jim that I first heard 'Because I Love You'. It was the second night of the long solo drive from Queensland and I had booked into a motel in Jerilderie, near the border of NSW and Victoria. In the room, I turned on the TV and the Lee Jeans commercial caught my eye. That was the first time I heard the song that would be the soundtrack to the next 26 years of my life with Jim. Family legend has it that my great grandmother was in Jerilderie at the time of the Kelly Gang hold up, so, oddly enough, it is a memorable place in both of our lives.

*

Within 24 whirlwind hours, I was at Snezana's family home, getting ready to go out. The plan was to pick up Juno Roxas and head over to Jim's so we could meet and I could see the house. Juno was the larger-than-life lead singer of Roxus, an up and coming band at the time that was widely tipped to be the next big thing.

As we walked in darkness up the path to the front door, we passed an older couple coming out. Snezana said hi to them and told me it was Jim's mum and stepfather. I couldn't really see them in the darkness and didn't think too much of the whole event that was unfolding. Here I was, at the front door of my future home, about to meet my future husband, with my future parents-in-law and my soul-sister Snezana. And my main concern was still my beloved car. I fancy the Universe looking upon that scene and taking a cosmic snapshot – *click!* – of a moment in time when soul paths converge at the one pivotal point to change the course of history.

The house looked nice, from what I could see in the darkness, with a double garage to the left! Perfect! Suddenly, I felt nervous standing there on the porch as the doorbell rang. What if he didn't like me?

The door opened and there stood a man in green pixie boots. Pixie boots! I suppose I had been expecting a sixties singer to look like an old hippie, but this guy looked more like my all-time favourite music idol, Rod Stewart, crossed with a member of Status Quo! More seventies rock than sixties hippie.

Clearly feeling right at home, Juno greeted Jim and sauntered in as Snezana introduced us. To my dismay, he was almost off-hand and after we all went into the lounge room and sat down, I realised that Jim was virtually ignoring me whilst talking to everyone else. The conversation bounced around, but Jim never looked at me or spoke to me, almost to the point of rudeness.

After a while, he left the room to go upstairs and dress to go out. Snezana went with him. I heard her call my name, so I went in search of her and found her in the foyer. The house was sprawling, with four bedrooms, a study, four reception rooms and three bathrooms. The colour scheme was a very eighties palette of palest pink and honey brown, which I liked.

Snezana asked me what I thought of the house, and I replied, "It's great but I don't think I'll be living here. I get the feeling Jim doesn't like me."

Snezana looked at me in utter disbelief.

"Are you kidding?" she half-whispered, "We were just talking about you, and he thinks you're absolutely *gorgeous*!"

Part of me wondered how I could have got it so wrong. Another part of me wondered how he could even know what I looked like when he had barely glanced at me! Later, Jim would tell me that he was pole-axed when he opened the door because, for him, it was love at first sight. He waggled his fingers at me like a magician casting a spell and said, "You were so stunning, I didn't know where to look! Couldn't you feel the electricity in the air? It was all around!"

\*

That night was the first of many out on the town in vibrant Melbourne. Regularly voted 'The World's Most Livable City', Melbourne had a heart and soul to it like no other. New York and London are the only other cities I have visited with a similar feel. Wherever we went, Jim would almost always turn up and Snezana later told me that Jim had been calling her to find out where we were going each night. We got along so well that I began to look for him and felt disappointed if he didn't show. He was funny and interesting and before long a time was made for me to meet him at the house to discuss the requirements of tenancy.

I went over one evening and we sat and talked about all manner of things. Jim was one of the most intelligent men I had ever met, with a wealth of general knowledge and a great vocabulary. He loved to play with words and so do I. Our conversations were free ranging, liberally interspersed with puns and corny jokes. We talked for hours.

Eventually I broached the subject of renting the room. I really needed to find a place to live and soon. Snezana's family were happy for me to stay but I did not want to impose upon their generosity much longer.

"There is a problem," began Jim, and my heart sank, "and that is, that I want to go out with you. I'm reluctant to take you on as a tenant. I've had problems in the past with female boarders developing feelings for me, so I am really looking for a male tenant."

It was not what I had expected at all but I already knew Jim well enough to be myself so I spoke frankly in the way of a true Sagittarian.

"Well, you don't need to worry about that because I'm not interested in getting involved with anyone. You know I'm going to be travelling overseas with Snezana in a few months plus I'm already in love with somebody, anyway."

Jim simply looked at me and quietly asked, "Well, where is he?"

That was a very good question. I'd been in love with a man for some time but he was one of this world's truly free spirits. He was also the best looking man I'd ever seen. A man so beautiful that he never had to choose one woman unless he wanted to. We never had a fight or a falling out but I had come to accept that he would never be fully present in my life. It wasn't enough for me and it was time to move on. My heart was broken but I looked forward to the future and to living my dream of travelling the world.

That seemed to settle it for Jim and he said it was too late to be driving back to Snezana's and that I may as well stay the night and move my things over tomorrow. He showed me to the room that would be mine and I slept for the first time in my new home.

*

Life was busy and exhilarating. Working in the heart of such a vibrant city, every day was an adventure. There was always something on in the evening – dinner, a gig, a party and clubs like Chasers, Chevron and The Metro. I soon made new friends amongst my colleagues, and we would sometimes head out to city clubs after work. Life was action-packed and fun!

Being a newbuild, the big pink house had no window coverings and it was like living in a fishbowl with vast expanses of glass on the east and west fronts. There was a serious lack of privacy. Jim hadn't wanted to skimp on quality, nor did he have the funds for professionally fitted curtains, so he found a temporary solution of crepe paper curtains, which were stapled to the frames.

I'd also noticed that there was no washing machine, dryer or mop. When I had my first full load of washing, I asked Jim for directions to the nearest laundromat. I watched, mystified, as Jim proceeded to pile all of his washing, and mine – clothes, towels and bed linen – into bags. Then we drove across town to a laundromat in Williams Road, Prahran. Incidentally, this was the laundromat I used to walk to each week when I was nineteen and rented in the same street.

Jim left the laundry to be done, paying $50 for a serviced wash and dry! In 1988, I considered that to be an outrageous waste of money and pointed out that a cheap washing machine would pay for itself in a few weeks' worth of these washes. Jim had never had a washing machine and we bought a new one on sale the following week. I had to teach him how to use it, but it was a revelation to him, like a kid gaining a small independence. I still smile remembering his enthusiasm for loading up the machine and pegging the laundry out to dry in the sun.

*

Jim was on tour when Juno called and asked if I'd like to go with him to the David Lee Roth concert. That was the first time I met Ian 'Molly' Meldrum. I knew that he was one of Jim's oldest and dearest friends, but I'd never met Molly until Juno introduced us. My sister, Petrina (Trina), and I had grown up watching *Countdown* but we had to be sneaky about it as our dad would switch off the TV whenever he found us watching something he deemed inappropriate. An Angus Young guitar solo was guaranteed to do it. One of my most vivid *Countdown* memories was of Trina and I, utterly transfixed by a new band called Van Halen covering 'You Really Got Me'. Eddie Van Halen in all his gorgeousness, God rest his soul, might have been okay, but our dad walked in just as the camera zoomed in on the lead singer. With flowing blonde locks and a red satin shirt wide open, displaying washboard abs that disappeared into the lowest-slung leather pants we'd ever seen, he was executing a perfect figure eight pelvic grind into the camera when Dad walked in. Done. TV off. Ten years on, I could hardly believe I was watching a David Lee Roth concert, from a corporate box, with Molly Meldrum!

More often than not, I'd arrive home from work in the afternoon to find Jim sitting at the table eating his breakfast cereal in his white terry-towelling dressing gown, legs crossed, a tousled mane of hair, face unshaven, reading the daily news. Jim read the newspaper from front to back every single day before doing the cryptic crossword and general knowledge quiz.

He'd look up and give me the biggest smile, ask me about my day and set about making me a cup of tea while he listened to the day's goings on in retail fashion. I found it endearing that Jim loved a cup of tea and always asked me if I would like one when he put the kettle on.

Being Jim's tenant was highly entertaining. If he was home, friends would drop in and they'd sit around talking and listening to music late into the night. Jim's lifestyle was nocturnal and, if I wasn't out and about, I'd leave them to it and get to bed so I wasn't too tired for work the next day.

There was also a constant stream of women from all walks of life, mostly calling on the phone and occasionally turning up at the house. This was the eighties, so no mobile phones; just the landline on the wall in the kitchen. I would answer if Jim didn't. Most of them seemed to view me as some sort of threat, which I found vastly amusing. My mind was still set on travelling at this point. Some were overtly hostile on the phone, and there was one girl who would call incessantly. She even followed us home from clubs late at night a few times and parked out front of the house.

Jim's cat, Ricky, was the biggest, most rotund cat I had ever seen, which was in total contrast to his soft, timid nature. I loved him immediately. When Jim went away on tour with Masters Apprentices, he would call each day ostensibly to check on the house, mail and Ricky. Once those topics were covered, instead of saying goodbye and getting back to the life of a rock legend on the road, Jim would find all manner of reasons to keep me talking on the phone. The conversations carried on just as they did when we were together and the calls would end hours later. With the benefit of hindsight, I later realised that Jim had started a slow courtship or, at the very least, a subtle seduction, but I didn't know that at the time.

I found myself looking forward to those daily phone calls more and more, which was slightly baffling. It felt like I was talking for hours with my best friend. Time would tell because, as it turned out, I was. I remember vividly the moment I realised that I had fallen for Jim because it was really confusing to me. I was lying in bed trying to get to sleep and failing dismally. My heart felt really strange, like it was moving inside me and trying to reach out of my chest. My heart was reaching out for Jim, which I kept telling myself was ridiculous. Lying there, tossing and turning, admonishing myself with all sorts of stern, get-a-grip self-talk, I reminded myself of my reason for being in Melbourne at all. Snezana and I were going to travel the world and I would be leaving Jim behind. He would carry on with his life and I would be living my dream. So why were there tears on my cheeks and why was my heart hurting?

One night, Snezana and I were out in the car, driving through the city, dressed to kill, when I suddenly burst into tears. "What's wrong?" she asked, looking alarmed, and I wailed, "I think I'm in love with Jim!"

Snezana roared with laughter, "That's great! What are you crying for?"

"Because I want to go overseas with you!" I sobbed.

There's a lot to be said for a man who remains present. Since flagging his desire to date me, and me shutting him down, Jim had been the perfect landlord and gentleman. He'd never raised the subject again or made any sort of move on me but when he was not on tour, he always invited me out with him whenever he had something on. When we came home, we'd drink cups of tea and sit up late into the night talking, then go to our separate rooms. The ball was in my court, but did I really want to return serve? In my heart, I already knew the answer was yes.

Thanks to Jim, who chased down copies of every photo taken when we were out and about, there's a beautiful framed black and white photo of us sitting in the back seat of a vintage convertible. Jim has his arm around me in a this-is-my-girl sort of way and we are all aglow with happiness. I call it the photo of our first date but really, it was the night I decided it was time to return serve.

Jim had asked me weeks earlier if I'd like to go with him to the opening night of a venue in the city. It was a red carpet event and Jim had said to dress up, so I did, choosing a designer dress that I'd brought with me from the Gold Coast. It was high eighties glamour in black and gold, a figure-hugging strapless dress with a corseted bustier and a slit pencil skirt. The pièce de résistance was the black taffeta panniered overskirt, handpainted with gold. Teamed with black patent stiletto heels, heavy gold jewellery, hot pink lipstick and my blue-black, Cher-inspired hair, I was pretty happy with the result. By the look on Jim's face as I descended the staircase, red carpet ready, I knew I'd got it right. He looked like he'd just won the lottery.

\*

By November, Jim and I were definitely a couple and I flew over to Adelaide after finishing work one Saturday to join him at the Formula One Grand Prix. Jim was performing that night in the Rock of Ages concert where we met up with Jim's mum and stepfather, Nancy and Sam.

In postwar Scotland, Nancy had been a young, unmarried mother, pressured into giving her baby son up for adoption, 'for the good of the child'. From the moment she handed Jim over, she regretted it and searched relentlessly for him for forty years before finally tracking him down in Australia. Jim and Jessie Keays, Jim's adoptive parents, had passed away years earlier so Jim felt no conflict of loyalty. Not only was he the spitting image of his mother, they got along from the moment they first spoke on the phone. Jim felt fortunate to have regained his natural mother, Nancy, along with her wonderful husband, Sam.

The next day, we watched the race with Sam from the entertainment platform and my beer drinking education began. I'd liked Jim's Scottish stepdad from the moment we met. Everyone liked Sam; he was that sort of guy. Anyway, it was a hot day and Sam asked if I'd like a drink. After some discussion about the merits of water versus beer on a hot day, I agreed to try a beer with my water. I'd never liked beer but took a sip of this one so as not to offend Sam.

When Sam asked, "What do you think of that beer?" honesty compelled me to say that I didn't really like the flavour.

"That's because you're sipping it like a girl, dear," he said. "Beer needs to hit the back of the palate, not the front of your tongue. So, take a good mouthful and get it straight to the back of your throat."

It sounded a bit rude to me but after some coaching on the art of taking a good swig, I was starting to enjoy the beer. In retrospect, I think it had as much to do with the drinking companion as the beer because beer never tasted as good as when I was having a pint with Sam. And we had a few over the years.

Jim always said he knew I was the one he'd been waiting for from the moment he opened his front door, and he proposed very quickly. For me, it felt like a whirlwind and I was deeply in love but sometimes I wondered if I was being rushed into something so important. Whenever I checked in with my heart, though, the thought of leaving him behind was unbearable.

We went shopping for a ring and found the perfect one at a jeweller in Doncaster shopping centre, which we put on lay by. We had shopped around a lot – I'd been to all the jewellers in the city in my lunch breaks – but we had narrowed it down to two from the same shop: a teardrop ruby or an oval sapphire. I couldn't decide and when Jim said he liked the sapphire because it matched my eyes, the choice was made. The style was a much smaller version of Lady Diana's ring, small diamonds surrounding a sapphire in a lighter shade of blue.

*

Masters Apprentices and their entourage were staying at a hotel in Broadbeach for their South East Queensland dates in December. Jim had already met my parents for the first time, quite by accident, while he was across the road at Pacific Fair shopping centre having lunch at a café. My parents walked past and thought they recognised their future son-in-law from the photos in the newspaper. Deciding that there could only be one man with that mane of hair, they went on in and introduced themselves!

When I arrived to visit Jim at the hotel, walking along looking at room numbers, there were three girls ahead, hanging around on the balconied walkway, so I had an inkling I was getting close. As I approached, I could see them checking me out and whispering. Sure enough, as I sailed past nonchalantly, there was Jim's room number. Opening the door, I stepped inside and snapped it closed in their frantic faces.

We spent the Christmas period on the Gold Coast with my family and while we were there, Jim asked my father for his permission to marry me. My family was delighted. Everybody liked Jim, even my grandpa, who had five granddaughters and notoriously high expectations of any man they brought home to meet him. Jim had very long hair at that time, and it had been with a fair amount of trepidation that I introduced them. Thankfully, they got along like a house on fire. Grandpa later told me that he liked Jim very much. "He has a good face," he said.

Christmas Day 1988 was epic. The Masters had worked the night before so I was to pick up Jim from the hotel and bring him home for the traditional family Christmas. Before that, though, I'd planned a special gift for my new fiancé. Up bright and early, hair and makeup done, I put on my lingerie, Jim's favourite on me, a black lace corset with suspenders. My mum, surprisingly, didn't bat an eyelid when I asked for her help in tying an enormous red bow around my waist. Then, covered from neck to knee in my sister's black evening cape, I cruised up the Gold Coast Highway in Mum's old HD Holden, parked in the hotel basement and walked to the lift. It was very early, about 7:30 am, and I'd planned it that way to avoid running into any of the band or crew. Unfortunately, my plan was foiled by the tour manager who got into the lift with me. I couldn't believe it!

This tour manager had been hired for his professionalism after his predecessor had absconded with the tour profits. However, the band had been known to remark on what they perceived as a lack of rock'n'roll consciousness in their tour manager! We said hi and little else as the lift went up, but I knew he must have been suspicious about why I was wrapped in a black cape, wearing high heels and fishnet stockings at that time of the morning on Christmas Day. I found myself struggling to keep a straight face. The lift opened on Jim's floor, not a moment too soon, and I walked to Jim's room, quietly letting myself in to surprise him with his Christmas present. Did he like it? Let's just say I never saw Jim unwrap a gift as enthusiastically as he did that morning.

We spent our first Christmas together at the Currumbin Valley banana farm that my grandparents had bought decades before. By this time, Uncle Brian and Auntie Margaret were living there and my dad travelled daily to and from our family home in Burleigh Heads to work on the farm. My sister, Trina, and I grew up closely with our three beautiful cousins, Amanda, Niaomi and Lyndall, spending school holidays on the farm with them. The huge family Christmas lunch was set up on the verandah, shaded by towering Jacarandas and overlooking the creek with pristine rainforest beyond. Auntie Margaret was, and still is, a wonderful host, and the long festive table was laden with a mix of traditional and tropical Christmas fare. After lunch, we changed into our swimmers and recovered from the food coma in the pool, floating about on a li-lo, or lounging around the edge and chatting desultorily. Jim absolutely loved being part of our big family, loved chatting with the girls and their partners, my grandparents, uncle and aunt, and my parents. It was new to him, being an integral part of such a large, loving family, but he fit right in.

*

The 1988/1989 Masters Apprentices reunion tour continued and one hot, summer's afternoon, Jim picked me up straight from work in Melbourne to drive to that night's gig at Collendina. We had to be there early as they were shooting a film clip for the new single, 'Birth of the Beat'. The filming was being done by Salik Silverstein, the video director who'd also filmed the clip for the 1988 recording of 'Because I Love You'. I enjoy that film clip more now for its historical value because it's a collage of unscripted, impromptu snippets of footage from soundcheck through to the live gig that night and all the waiting around in between. It's a genuine snapshot of a typical day's work in the life of a touring rock band in the 1980s. There's a quick shot of me at the start holding the blue top I'd worn to work, twirling around in a black dress as Jim walks towards me. We were in the pub's squash court, where I changed out of my work clothes. The band room was in the sports complex; no green room there, so I needed to improvise and found a semi-private spot behind a door, where I changed while Jim stood guard. I'd just finished and was asking Jim if I looked okay when Salik walked in and caught the moment with his camera.

Unfortunately, the camera didn't catch a shot of whoever it was that stole the large box containing the band's tour merchandise from the back of the truck behind the gig. Jim heard later that someone was seen selling Masters Apprentices reunion tour t-shirts at a market somewhere in Melbourne. He was so used to people stealing his clothes from band rooms and hotel rooms over the years that he just shrugged it off because none of those many thefts bothered him as much as the theft of the first Masters Apprentices' drummer's Dad's cricket blazer in the sixties, which Jim wore on stage, and Jim's own Masters Apprentices studded leather tour jacket, specially designed and handmade for him by a friend in the eighties. He had another leather jacket made but went to his death never feeling at peace about the loss of either item.

Not long after Jim and I became engaged, one of the women from Jim's past crossed the line and went from weird to vengeful when she went into my workplace on my day off and made a complaint against me. Management followed up the complaint, presumably as she intended. It was easily explained to my employers, but I was mortified to have been put in that position.

Although the intent was spiteful at best, that ugly little episode forced me to really look at what had occurred and why. Jim and I were engaged to be married, yet the same list of women continued to call for various reasons. Often, it was to invite Jim out or just to maintain contact. Sometimes, it was to ask for money. None of them expressed any interest in getting to know me and being part of our life together, and Jim didn't consider them his friends, anyway.

Jim's easygoing nature was one of the things about him that I loved most but it was apparent that he had a complete lack of healthy boundaries. Part of that was down to his innately rebellious nature but most of it was probably due to all the years he'd spent as part of a touring rock band, where everything was done for him and someone else handled all the unpleasant stuff. My mother-in-law once told me about an incident at Jim's house when she was staying with him in Carlton. He never locked his front door and two women had arrived uninvited within minutes of each other and started a catfight. Nancy walked in to find the two women in the lounge room screeching and yelling at each other while Jim was crouched in the corner of the couch. It was up to Nancy to intervene and throw them both out, which I imagine happened pretty quickly. My mother-in-law may have been a tiny lady but she was not one to be messed with.

So, Jim and I had possibly our first talk addressing a serious issue that had the potential to affect our relationship. Feeling safe in my own home was non-negotiable for me. If these people weren't our friends, if they did not wish us well as a couple, then there was no place for them in our home – either physically or by telephone. I had only recently started to become aware of the precarious state of Jim's finances, too. When I agreed to marry him, it really was for better or worse, richer or poorer and I was in it for the long haul. However, it was not my job to set the boundaries here, it was Jim's, and I waited to see what would happen. To his credit, Jim proceeded to deal with each intrusion as it occurred, calmly and firmly explaining that we would be married and there was no longer any reason for their calls nor any place for them in our life. Of course, to some of them it was like a red rag to a bull and their behaviour escalated. Some days, there would be over 20 silent hang-up calls. Thankfully, once the Telco became involved in monitoring the nuisance phone calls, things settled down.

*

The year flew by as our wedding plans came together. My dad had opened investment accounts for my sister and me when we were born, specifically to pay for our weddings. As unbelievable as it sounds today, we had a budget of $2000 and that is exactly what we brought the wedding in at, except for my dress. I knew exactly what I wanted for my dress, but it was a vision in my mind and not in any shop. A colleague introduced me to her friend who had worked for a high-end wedding designer, and she offered to make the dress for me. Every detail was sketched and refined until, finally, the image in my head was before me on paper. Every detail was perfect, from the luxurious ivory duchess satin to the delicate crystal and pearl design embroidery. Over several months, I went for fittings, paying progress instalments from my wages until the day came when I took home the beautiful, bespoke wedding gown of my dreams. Jim loved classic Jaguar cars so these were chosen as the mode of transport for the bridal party. Even my bouquet was designed exactly as I dreamed it would be.

We were married in the Spring of 1989 at Montsalvat, an artist colony outside of Melbourne set in idyllic grounds. Built early in the 1900s of local stone, Montsalvat could be a medieval village in the French countryside. Small but beautiful, our wedding was held in the stone chapel and the reception was a medieval style banquet set in the Great Hall. Some aspects were traditional, and others were very definitely rock and roll, including the wedding video, which was filmed by our friend, producer Salik Silverstein. Nineteen eighty-nine was the year of the pilot strike in Australia, so flying wasn't an option and only my immediate family had arranged for enough time off to drive from the Gold Coast to Melbourne for the wedding. My dad's cousins, who made the drive from the NSW Riverina, were the only other family members on my side. Dad walked me down the aisle and my sister, Petrina, was my bridesmaid.

We'd hired a juke box for dance music and it was set up in the Great Hall. To our great amusement, Sigmund Jörgensen – the owner of the venue – referred to it as 'the beast'. For our bridal waltz, we'd chosen the Mink DeVille song, 'So In Love Are We'. Jim had brought along his vinyl album with the song on it and he'd arranged for it to be played on the record player at the venue, which we tested in the days prior and was working perfectly. When the time came for us to take to the dance floor, we stood waiting a few moments only to be told, "It doesn't work! The needle's stuffed."

Quick as a flash, our friend and guitarist, the inimitable Wayne 'Morry' Matthews, jumped up and crossed to the juke box, calling out, "Don't worry! I'll pick something!"

Jim and I, who were already nervous enough about dancing in front of our friends, looked at each other in trepidation and then laughed as the first notes of 'Because I Love You' filled the Great Hall. It wasn't what we had planned but, in retrospect, it couldn't have been more perfect.

Snezana could not be there for our wedding, but I understood why. She had watched Jim and I fall in love and foreseen the inevitable. Our dream of travelling the world together was not going to happen and she had left on her own for Japan, where she was already establishing her career as an internationally renowned DJ.

There she found her own great love story when she met and fell in love with her future husband, Logan. Tall, gorgeous, with male model looks and a mane of blonde hair that any woman would envy, Logan was the perfect partner for my free-spirited Sagittarian soul sister. True Love will always find its way.

## Chapter Two

# Pressure Makes Diamonds

*"As soon as you trust yourself, you will know how to live."*
*~ Johann Wolfgang von Goethe*

By 1994, we were, for the first time in our marriage in a stable financial position. And together as a couple, we'd worked hard to get there. The recession and property crash of the late 1980s and early 1990s had seen us almost lose everything. The government wanted to cool the boom and home loan interest rates were over 17%. The entertainment industry is always one of the first to suffer in an economic recession and live work had dried up. Jim had built the house in East Doncaster intending to turn it over quickly in the booming property market and had a mortgage along with several other loans and debts. As interest rates soared, we were unable to meet the monthly repayments, even with both of our incomes.

The big pink house was sold as we watched property prices plummet further each day and interest rates sky-rocket. We counted ourselves lucky that we managed to sell at all, because buyers were scarce and the bank was breathing down Jim's neck.

It was sad leaving the house where we met and fell in love, but the beautiful Victorian villa that we bought in East St Kilda was a happy home, too. Only a short walk away from the vibrant shopping strip of Carlisle Street, Balaclava, we soon settled into the cooler, more urban lifestyle. Financially, it was still a struggle as the recession continued to drag on. It was a terrible time in Australian political history that saw many families and businesses lose everything. My pride and joy, the little red Laser, was also sold to help meet the mortgage repayments.

It may not sound like an ideal start to married life, but I remember those times as being filled with love, fun and laughter. We even had our own language, developed from constant wordplay, and could hold an entire conversation that only we understood. Admittedly, those conversations were often ridiculously funny nonsense, but that's what we loved about it! Certainly, there were difficult times, but they came from outside sources and were mainly financial. As a couple, we stayed strong and always turned towards each other, rather than away, when faced with adversity. We also had what Jim called 'our ESP' going on, often knowing what the other was thinking without having to say a word. Through years of major life tests that had seen many a marriage falter, we emerged on the other side closer than ever.

We lived our marriage mindful of each other's happiness, being all for one and one for all. Two people with shared goals, working towards them as one, while supporting each other in our personal goals and trying to make the other happy.

Like the time Jim organised tickets for us to see Rod Stewart and I got to see my all-time idol in concert for the first time. I've loved Rod Stewart since the age of 13 when my cousins gave me the album *Footloose and Fancy Free* for Christmas. There was no turning back for me from that day forward and I have loved him since with the same sort of adoration and devotion I've seen for Jim from his fans over the years. Sometimes people would ask me if it worried me, watching women old enough to know better falling over themselves to speak with Jim, to kiss him and have their photo taken with him. But I totally get it. I only hope that if I ever have the privilege of meeting Sir Rod Stewart, I can utter something vaguely intelligible. Needless to say, I did not get to meet Rod Stewart that night, despite Jim's best efforts, but I'll never forget the feeling of seeing my idol live for the first time, of crying, smiling and laughing with Jim by my side.

As if the recession wasn't devastating enough, in 1991 the Victorian government legalised poker machines in pubs and venues across the state. The impact on the music industry was immediate, a coup de grâce to musicians with many venues doing away with live music altogether and the remainder offering only the bare minimum required by law.

Jim had been a professional musician since Masters Apprentices came to fame in the mid-sixties. Decades of working in his chosen profession as a pioneer of Australian music saw him well-placed to weather the industry drought with his indisputable talent, strong work ethic and an extensive body of work in both song writing and performance holding him in good stead. Where many were forced to leave music behind and take 'day jobs', Jim continued to earn a living doing what he loved.

Jim was constantly working, putting forward proposals for TV shows, gigs, recordings and films. Some came through, but a lot did not. Such is the industry. During this period, he wrote and recorded a song for the environment called 'Our Children's World', – which was prompted by the news of a hole in the ozone layer at the time – negotiating its release through Virgin Records. Amongst the long list of projects always on the go, there was 'Guru of Pop', a rap song about his old friend, Molly Meldrum, in between hustling gigs and weekly song writing sessions in our lounge room. If it was a lean month, Jim would make a few phone calls and hustle up a few celebrity DJ gigs to fill in the gaps. He didn't love those jobs, but he always did what was needed to pay the bills.

In my opinion, Jim's relentless drive and work ethic over all the years was the major force in keeping the name of Masters Apprentices alive. Without Jim's public profile, professionalism and tireless work, the band would have faded into history as so many of its contemporaries did. Most of the early band members left the music industry altogether when they left the band. None of them maintained a high profile, apart from Glenn Wheatley, who was on a different path altogether at that time with a highly successful international career in management and media.

Five years on, I'd moved from fashion retail to business development with a major transport company. My role was secure, I was earning and contributing as much as Jim, my colleagues were great and I enjoyed my work. Jim had written and recorded his third solo album, *Pressure Makes Diamonds*, which he dedicated to me. We had a close circle of good friends and entertained most weekends. The little home in the working-class northern suburb of Thornbury that we bought after the recession was slowly transforming. We worked together on weekends and at night painting, sewing curtains and creating a pretty cottage garden with the help of my parents, who visited regularly. Jim used to say he was born in the Year of the Dog and that, like a dog, he loved hearth and home.

One of Jim's songwriting partners on *Pressure Makes Diamonds* was also co-producer, Frank Sablotny. Jim and Frank were signed by the same music publisher, and it was that publisher who suggested that Jim and Frank should collaborate. The songwriting partnership produced a string of beautiful songs, including the magnificent 'Waiting for the Big One' and, once again, Jim made sure my legs made a cameo appearance in that film clip, too.

Frank and his wife, Liz, lived two streets away from us and we all clicked from the start. Hardly a week passed without at least one catch-up for a meal, taking it in turns to host at our homes. The dinner parties from that time have become the stuff of legend, now fondly remembered as 'Cardiology nights'. They started innocently enough, typically a three-course meal, always accompanied by great dinner music and conversation but, once the table was cleared, it was a different story. Jim would break out the deck of cards and deal a game of 500 (Cardiology), dinner music was replaced by The Cult turned up to 11, a bottle of red (tea for Jim) appeared, along with an ashtray and the lights were dimmed. In a haze of smoke, laughter and blisteringly loud rock music, those games would continue long into the night, growing evermore raucous as the hours passed.

Jim quietly announced one day that he'd looked at the budget and he thought we could afford to take a holiday to England, maybe go to Paris as well. I was at first stunned, then beside myself with happiness. My lifelong dream of world travel had been willingly put aside when I accepted Jim's marriage proposal and Jim never forgot it. It was the first thing he thought of when we were in a position to afford it. I loved him even more for doing so, if that was possible.

The fun of the trip began long before we departed. Sherrin, my friend and colleague in logistics, and I commenced regular lunch meetings at Melbourne Airport, in anticipation. We would meet at an establishment with floor-to-ceiling glass windows overlooking the international departure gates. There we would sit, watching the big planes over coffee and almond croissants, savouring the smell of aviation fuel!

Jim and I decided to explore mainly England with a short side-trip to Paris rather than a whistle stop tour of Europe. This meant that we could spend more time visiting Jim's family. I wanted to spend more time in Europe, but Jim said he knew that I would love England, and time would prove him right. We spent hours each night poring over Jim's old British road atlas, planning our itinerary. That first trip to England – land of castles, streams, forests, stone circles and pubs, alive with history – I was like a kid in a candy store and we set a cracking pace… spawning the self-proclaimed title of 'tourists extraordinaire'. It was my dream come true, made all the more magic for sharing the experience with Jim. The precious memories created will stay with me for life and I know they stayed with Jim. Throughout our life together, we would often reminisce about our travels, reminding each other of little moments in time. In Jim's last days, he would wait for me to arrive at the hospital and greet me with something like, "Hey Darl, remember that day when we drove into Bath for the first time? Your face! I'll never forget the look on your face when we drove down the hill and first saw it!"

Walking through Myer Melbourne a few days before we left, it occurred to me that a good book would be handy to have on the flight. I was working, in a hurry, and my eye fell upon a weighty paperback novel with a castle, sword, crown and sunset on the cover. Four of my favourite things! I picked it up, paid for it and continued on. It wasn't until I was on the plane that I looked at the back cover blurb to find that I had chosen a book about the Wars of the Roses, a period in England's medieval history that I knew little about. *The Sunne in Splendour* by Sharon K Penman is meticulously researched and the plot is set within the framework of documented history. Throughout that long flight, the story of Richard III and the House of York began to unfold, the characters coming alive to me, and I realised that I would be going to some of the very same places where these people had lived and died and where the events I was reading about had actually taken place over 500 years ago.

QANTAS flight QF9, my first long-haul plane trip in economy class, touched down at Heathrow Airport at 5:30 am towards the end of July. Sleep-deprived and in dire need of a shower, we took the airport train to the city and a London cab to the Columbia Hotel in Lancaster Gate. Jim had booked us a room there for five nights as he'd stayed there previously when recording in Britannia Row studios. The Columbia is a rock'n'roll hotel, a grand Georgian building filled with original period features of faded glory and very definitely not five star, not even four, but we loved it. Set on Bayswater Road, directly opposite Hyde Park and close to the tube, Paddington and Notting Hill, it was a great spot to stay when in London. We dropped our luggage in the storage room and headed off into the early morning. It was probably the quietest I've ever seen London; the street sweepers were out and the shops weren't yet open. We wandered around and found ourselves in a beautiful square of the greenest, manicured grass and gardens overlooked on all sides by rows of splendid Georgian townhouses, older than any architecture I'd ever seen before. There was a statue of an historical figure mounted high on a plinth in the square and, as I read the plaque on the base, that is where I first felt an intense surge of homecoming that took my breath away. It felt as though the energy of this place and all that came before me shot up through my feet and every cell in my body rejoiced. It was completely unexpected and hit me like an electric shock. Britain had never been high on my travel wish list. Like many fifth generation Australians, I was raised with a slight disdain for all things English. In time, I came to understand it was the inherited result of the grief and anger of many families, my own included, who had seen their young men volunteer to fight under the command of the British forces in World War 1 and never return.

Apart from wanting to see Nancy and Sam again, I had been ambivalent about going there up until that point, but as I stood in that beautiful London square with tears of joy in my eyes and my heart bursting with gratitude, it occurred to me that family ancestry might be more than just words on a birth certificate. I may be in the fifth generation of my family in Australia, but untold generations of my ancestors had lived and died in the British Isles and my body felt as though it had plugged into that energy and was being recharged.

Jim couldn't resist a little "I told you so" before taking me for my first ride on a London double-decker bus, the hop on, hop off guided tour buses that stop at all the major tourist attractions in the capital. We were tired so we stayed on the bus, sitting on the open top deck in the summer sunshine, listening to the commentary from the tour guide. It was a great way for me to get my bearings in one of the greatest cities and I gazed wide-eyed as we rode past the most legendary of places. Buckingham Palace, Trafalgar Square, Fleet Street, Hyde Park, Tower of London, Tower Bridge all appeared before me. It felt surreal and at the same time, I had never felt more alive.

Back at the Columbia Hotel, we settled into our room filled with magnificent original Georgian period features including the enormous marble fireplace. Double-hung sash windows opened out over the portico and we would step out onto the roof and sit there taking in the sunshine and vibes before crossing the road to Hyde Park. As a teenager, I devoured romance novels by Georgette Heyer and Barbara Cartland. Hyde Park and Rotten Row were almost mythical to me. With each step I took in this vibrant city, I felt the energy of the countless people who had stepped in that same spot before me over the centuries. I fell in love with London that day with a passion that has never waned.

Each night, usually after dinner at The Swan pub, we would settle into bed. Jim would watch TV and I would continue reading *The Sunne in Splendour* until my eyes could no longer remain open. As the story of the House of York unfolded before me, I would marvel that I had that day walked in the footsteps of these long-ago people, where they had lived, died and created history. I told Jim what I had learned, and he took it all in because he was a sponge when it came to knowledge. He loved seeing my enjoyment of London and my enthusiasm for its layers of history.

Five days later, we picked up our hire car and set out for Bath, stopping at Stonehenge on the way. As we drove through Somerset, the landscape changed and so did the villages. Thatched cottages with mullioned windows lined the roads, their roughcast walls dripping with wisteria and rambling roses. The nearer we got to Bath, the higher the hedgerows became on each side of the road, laden with berries, flowers, birds and bumblebees. I felt like I was in a fairytale land, and then we entered a stretch of road that was like a magic tunnel of trees such as I'd never seen before in Australia. They arched over the road, so green and graceful, allowing dappled sunlight to dance on the road ahead of us. It was all too beautiful to be true and I began to cry. The English countryside on a sunny summer's day looks exactly how I'd always imagined that Heaven would be. I felt like I'd found Heaven on Earth and the tears I shed were ones of pure joy.

We spent blissful days exploring the area around Bath, before meandering slowly north along the Welsh marches to Cheshire, staying in traditional B&Bs each evening. The day came when we drove into the Lakes District and I had my first glimpse of the glorious landscape that has inspired artists and writers for centuries. It was also the home of Jim's mum and Sam, along with his Uncle Bill and Aunt Elsie. Bill and Elsie lived near Grizedale Forest where Bill had been head forester for many years before setting up the Grizedale Society. As director of the Grizedale Society, Bill was the driving force behind the Theatre in the Forest which hosted many luminaries. Bill was a visionary and had a revolutionary idea that the forest was owned by the people and should be enjoyed by the people. He instigated two sculpture trails which wound through Grizedale Forest, becoming, at the time, one of the world's largest collections of sculpture in a natural setting. Famous sculptors, such as Andy Goldsworthy, and many up-and-coming artists, were invited to create sculptures in situ. Made of materials from the forest, they are designed to be enjoyed as they slowly break down over time and return to nature.

It was a magical time staying with Nancy and Sam, of going for walks and drives in one of the most beautiful places on Earth, of afternoon tea on the lawn at Bill and Elsie's, overlooking the lake with majestic mountains beyond. Bill took us on tours of the forest, arranging with Sam to meet us at local pubs for lunch. Usually, it would be their favourite, a 400-year-old inn full of character, called The Drunken Duck. Most days, Jim and Nancy would be sitting together with a pot of tea, and Sam would look at me with a raised eyebrow and point to the door. A nod from me and then we'd be off for a drive or a walk, which always involved stopping by at least one pub that I'd never been to before – just so I could sample their beer and give Sam my opinion.

We packed a lot into those four weeks, driving up to Scotland then back down to York where, once again, I was awestruck to be standing inside York Minster where Richard III and his Queen had attended church many times as Duke of Gloucester, before he was King. We walked the ancient medieval city walls, which are built on the foundations of Roman walls. I gazed in disbelief at

Micklegate Bar, a fortressed gate in the walls where the head of Richard's father had been mounted on a pike after being killed at the Battle of Wakefield, along with Richard's brother, Edmund. On our last days in England, we stayed in a medieval B&B deep in the countryside and explored Stratford Upon Avon, the birthplace of William Shakespeare.

On the very last day we went to Warwick Castle, a massive, intact medieval castle built alongside the picturesque River Avon. From the book, I knew Richard III had spent some of his childhood in the castle, in the household of the Earl of Warwick, who would become known as the Kingmaker. In 1994, the castle was owned by the Tussauds Group, of Madame Tussauds waxworks fame, and featured a tour of the medieval undercroft complete with the sights, smells and sounds of a medieval castle preparing for war. There was so much going on at Warwick that day, even a concourse of vintage and luxury cars parked on the island within the castle grounds in the middle of the River Avon, that we might easily have missed the last day of the Richard III Society's exhibition inside the castle itself. Tired but happy, we were strolling through the castle interior on our way to the carpark when I saw the sign for the visiting Richard III display.

There we lingered, gazing incredulously at artefacts from Richard III's lifetime over 500 years ago. It felt preordained, the cherry on top of the delicious icing on the scrumptious dream cake that was my first overseas holiday. The next day we crossed the English Channel, leaving behind the famous White Cliffs of

Dover, and spent three thrilling, hot, summer days and nights in Paris before boarding the long, exhausting flight back home to cold, dark mid-winter in Melbourne.

\*

Exactly when and why I first thought of babies, I don't remember. It sort of snuck up on me as though, with life so stable and so many dreams fulfilled, I could relax. What I do remember is, once the idea popped into my head, it seemed to trigger my maternal body clock, or maybe it was the other way around. Chicken or egg, excuse the pun, it didn't matter because, although I didn't know it yet, once that clock started ticking there was no going back.

Jim was happy to try for a baby if that was what I wanted… he loved kids and likened them to little gurus. I had a big green light from my husband and no real reason not to have children if I wanted to. Nevertheless, I thought about it for months because having babies had never before been on my list of life goals. I wondered if the ticking of my maternal body clock was something that might stop as suddenly and unexpectedly as it had started. Not wanting to rush into such an important decision and also considering the implications for my career, I bought a pregnancy book, began taking folic acid and modified my diet, just in case I decided to go ahead. I had been taking the pill for years and had never been pregnant so I had no way of being sure that I could conceive.

*

Later that year, we were back in Adelaide again for the 1994 Adelaide Grand Prix race entertainment with Russell Morris, Swanee, Mental as Anything and a host of other big-name acts. Backstage at the Rock of Ages concert, I was chatting with the wife of Jim's old friend, Adelaide radio identity David Day. Annette and I had liked each other immediately and had much in common, including the loud ticking of our maternal body clocks. It seemed that everywhere I went, babies were the topic of conversation!

One balmy Adelaide night, we wandered en masse from the hotel to an Italian restaurant in O'Connell Street, filling the al fresco seating on the footpath for an impromptu dinner. The food was great and the conversation even better when two Harley Davidsons pulled up in front of us at the traffic lights with their unmistakeable throbbing rumble. Normie Rowe jumped up and began talking with one of the riders as they pulled over to the kerb.

Normie crossed to where Jim and I were sitting and said he was going to take one of the bikes for a ride. The rider was a veteran who had served in Vietnam with Normie and he was happy for Normie to take his bike for a spin.

Normie turned to me and said, "Karin! I've arranged for you to go on the other bike. Would you like a Harley ride?" I was out of that seat like a flash! The bike in question was the most impressive motorbike I'd ever seen – a huge, black Harley Davidson with a silver-studded pillion seat that looked fit for a queen. The rider, a fearsome-looking dude with a big moustache, was a total gentleman and an excellent rider. Introducing himself as Muff, he handed me a helmet and helped me fasten it before showing me how to mount the bike. Then he pulled out into the traffic and we glided off into the warm, Adelaide night.

As a teenager, I'd ridden pillion on my friend's trail bike many times and loved nothing more than tearing down the Gold Coast Highway with the wind in my hair and the sun on my skin. A Harley Davidson, though, took the thrill of riding to a whole new level, so effortless that there was no need to hang on. Adelaide's parks and gardens slid by as the bike purred along and I could smell the scent of water sprinklers, of the damp earth. It felt like flying and when we eventually pulled up back at the restaurant, I wished I could go again.

Thanking my gracious chauffeur, I walked back to the table and couldn't wait to tell Jim about my first ride on a Harley Davidson. Jim looked at me strangely, then said, "Yeah, Normie said that chicks love Harleys. He said they get off on the vibration."

I rolled my eyes, thinking that was such a boy thing to say! For me, my first Harley ride had inspired only pure joy and exhilaration. I looked at the other guys looking at me and wondered if they thought the same thing as Jim. It didn't deter me from wanting another Harley ride though, but it would be many years before I got the chance.

## Chapter Three

# Bridges

*"Always laugh when you can, it is cheap medicine."*
*~ Lord Byron*

Towards the end of 1994, I decided to stop the pill, thinking that I would allow my body a few months to resume its natural cycle. I must have conceived within weeks. The changes in my body were immediate; I became super-tired and just felt different inside. My breasts, which had always been on the small side of average, suddenly became luscious and full!

By the time we arrived in Queensland to spend Christmas with my family, I was incapable of doing much more than sleep and eat. I remember my sister commenting on my amazing breasts and thinking that perhaps I should go see a doctor for a pregnancy test.

When I did, there was a tiny trace of blue in the positive marker and the GP wouldn't confirm pregnancy, merely saying that I should see my regular doctor when I returned to Melbourne. This was disappointing as I had been hoping to be able to give my family the good news while we were there. Masters Apprentices' first roadie, Neil McCabe, lived on the Gold Coast and we caught up with Neil and his wife, Pattie. I remember confiding to Pattie that I might be pregnant, which was the cause of much excitement as Neil and Jim had been friends since the sixties.

Being my first ever pregnancy test, I didn't know much about it. So, when I saw my regular doctor back in Melbourne, I took the test along to show her. She took one look at it and said there was no doubt it had been a positive result. She had me take another test to make sure I was still pregnant as it was only early days and I'll never forget that feeling of watching the test turn up positive… I was pregnant! Inside my tummy, a new life was growing. I was a mum!

Intuitively, I felt pregnancy and childbirth were not a condition to be 'doctored', simply a natural bodily process for which my body was perfectly designed, but I had no information about any alternatives to the standard hospital / obstetrician / midwife model.

Frank and Liz , our old friends from Cardiology nights, were also expecting their first child. Liz had decided to give birth at the Family Birth Centre at a public hospital in Carlton, which offered a midwife-led, non-interventionist alternative to the obstetrics ward. This sounded perfect to me, the best of both worlds, and after taking a tour of the facility Jim and I agreed that I would book in to give birth there.

I loved being pregnant, rarely felt nauseous and never in the morning. As the tiredness of the first trimester passed, I felt amazing. There was so much love and joy flowing between me and

Jim and our baby growing within my body. I began antenatal yoga classes, which proved invaluable when it came time to labour. I felt sure that the baby was a little girl and the 18-week ultrasound confirmed it. Once we knew, I began decorating the nursery, making up cream calico curtains and stencilling the walls in pink roses.

I was pregnant with Holly when I first met Kelly and Leah Ford. Kelly was married at the time to Jim's songwriting partner and guitarist in Masters Apprentices, Doug Ford, and Jim and I went round to visit them and meet baby Leah. I'll never forget the first time I met Leah and Kelly, who to this day still are like family to us. Leah looked like an angel, all peaches and cream complexion, with blue eyes and blonde hair. Kelly had dressed her in a little outfit with tiny pink rosebuds and she was the sort of baby you couldn't help but coo over. Kelly handed Leah to me and I kissed her soft hair as she sat on my pregnant belly when, all of sudden, I felt a mighty thump from within! Then another, and another! Holly was kicking Leah, playing with her even before she was born! Nothing has changed. The two girls look and act like sisters and have been best friends all their lives: another great Ford/Keays partnership.

The hospital was only a short stroll to Carlton's famous Lygon Street and all the wonderful Italian restaurants. We would attend antenatal classes in the evening then wander up to Lygon Street for dinner. It was at one of those antenatal classes that I first heard of Syntocinon. The midwives would arrange for a new mother to talk to the class about her own birth experience. The young woman who spoke to us that night had been labouring in the Family Birth Centre but had not progressed and was transferred to the ward. It was in the ward that her labour was augmented by a Syntocinon drip and she had gone on to give birth without further intervention.

The midwife asked her if she had an epidural and was astonished when she replied that she had no pain relief at all. The midwife went on to explain how Syntocinon-induced contractions were known to be more intense and painful than natural labour. I'm sure the other mums-to-be in the antenatal class felt the same as me, fervently hoping they would never be in the position of requiring medical intervention. As it turned out, at 11 days over the due date, I was booked in for the dreaded induction. However, thankfully, I went into labour naturally that day. I'll never know why, but I like to think it was taking a natural laxative (an old fashioned home remedy that was suggested to me by a midwife) that saved me from induction.

On the evening of 18 September 1995, it was me speaking about my birth experience as a brand-new mother to a fresh group of parents-to-be. I was a perfect advertisement for a midwife-led birth experience. Holly was born in a textbook, first-time labour of 7 hours and 57 minutes from start to finish. Just as I'd hoped, it was a drug-free, completely natural labour, apart from the episiotomy at the end. After an hour of pushing, the midwife suggested the cut to avoid tearing. I agreed, feeling nothing more than a slight sting, and Holly was born within minutes.

The skills that I learned at pregnancy yoga class really helped me during my labour. Understanding the need to stay centred and calm, and remembering the breathing techniques was paramount to me being able to remain in control of my own birth experience. I believe it helped me to follow the instructions of the midwives, especially when the time came to push.

When the midwife handed Holly to me I could feel the cord that still connected us warm and pulsing around my leg as I held her in my arms for the first time. My heart bloomed, bursting wide open in love and amazement at the sight and feel of her. Even covered in blood and mucus, at 9 lb 8 oz (4445 g), Holly was the biggest, healthiest, most beautiful newborn baby I had ever seen and, to my total bemusement, she was blonde!

Jim cut the cord and held Holly as I delivered the placenta, then we all got into bed, our own little family, where we cuddled, talked and marvelled at the precious new life we had made. Our beautiful baby girl was a Virgo, just like her Dad and her aunt. After a while, the nurse wheeled me away to have the episiotomy stitched, leaving Jim holding Holly in his arms looking proud and utterly besotted.

Nine months later, we travelled back to the UK for Holly's first visit with Nancy and Sam. Of course, they absolutely doted on their new granddaughter and, for Nancy, whose arms had ached for forty long years with emptiness and yearning for her lost baby, it was a time of profound healing. Bill and Elsie also delighted in the new addition to the family. Holly took to international travel with ease, sleeping, eating and generally doing everything with a smile on her face. Much to Sam's delight, she first crawled on the banks of Lake Windermere with her proud grandad watching over her.

It was on the nightmarish 14-hour last leg of the flight home that I first heard the news that my beloved AFL team, the Brisbane Bears, would merge with the Fitzroy Lions. My team, who I had followed since their beginning at Carrara Oval on the Gold Coast, had suffered the reputation of being the easy beats of the competition for a long time, as had Fitzroy. After years of hard work and recruiting, the Bears had only recently started to come good.

Sleep deprived in mid-flight, I didn't know what to think about this news of a merger.

Apparently, a lot of old Fitzroy supporters felt the same and some were very vocal in their rejection, abandoning their old club and switching allegiance to other Melbourne-based clubs rather than support a Brisbane-Fitzroy merger. With Fitzroy's long, proud club history, both Jim and I felt sad that some supporters felt that way. When he first moved to Melbourne, he'd followed the Demons because they had the same colours as Norwood, his club in Adelaide. Although he'd lived in Carlton for years and could easily have chosen to support them or the Adelaide Crows when they formed, he never wavered and stuck by his beloved Demons through thick and thin until the end of his life.

Soon after we arrived back from the UK, I caught up with our neighbour from a few doors down. Flo and her husband, Colin, had lived in the same house in Thornbury all their married lives. It was Flo who told me how she and Colin built their house and used to sit on the front fence watching the horse races across the other side of the road. Back then, there was nothing there but the old Fitzroy Racecourse. It took up the land between Woolton Avenue and Gadd Street on the western side of St Georges Road and, Flo informed me, was frequented by the gangster Sqizzy Taylor and his gang. It explained why the cream brick houses on the other side of Woolton Avenue were from a much later period than our 1920's weatherboard Californian bungalow. A kind, spritely woman with white hair and sparkling eyes, Flo was salt of the earth. She was also a lifelong Fitzroy supporter and greeted me, bubbling with excitement over the news of the merger of our teams. Fitzroy Football Club was one of the oldest teams in the VFL. If Flo was gracious and open-minded enough to embrace the merger of our teams so enthusiastically, who was I to do any less?

My favourite memory of Flo is of arriving back home from a walk one day to find her waiting for me at our front gate. Brandishing an envelope excitedly, she couldn't wait to show me her membership medallion as a foundation member of the Brisbane Lions Football Club.

Jim was a Melbourne Demons member, in a coterie group called the Tridents, which consisted of Melbourne supporters in the entertainment industry. Tridents were usually seated in the same area of the MCG as the team members who were not playing that day. One day, whilst heavily pregnant with Holly and following Jim to our seats, I misjudged the height of the cement step and fell hard on my hands and knees. All I could see were Melbourne team blazers leaping up from all directions to help me to my feet. Assuring them I was fine, burning with embarrassment, I took my seat as fast as I could beside Jim, who had been oblivious to the whole thing with his back turned. I'd protected my belly, but my hands, knees and shins were grazed, black and blue for weeks.

Being avid footy supporters, we usually went to every Melbourne game for both teams, which sometimes meant seeing two games a week unless they clashed, in which case we went to our respective games alone. One dismal winter's day, I drove alone to Kardinia Park and sat in the outer in freezing cold rain to watch as the Geelong Cats decimated us. It got so bad that the Cats supporters around me were almost apologetic. It was a long drive home, but that's footy.

At the time, I was one of only six paid-up Brisbane Bears members in Melbourne so both Jim and I were well known to the Bears' Melbourne manager, Kinnear Beatson. Kin called me one day to ask if Jim could help. The newly formed Brisbane Lions would need new lyrics for their club anthem. The music would be the old Fitzroy tune of La Marseillaise, which is the French national anthem. The club had stipulated a few words that they wanted incorporated into the lyrics, but it was nowhere near a full song and, as a football club, songwriting was out of their league. I didn't even need to ask Jim. I just said yes for him!

Jim set to work on writing the lyrics for my club's anthem, then went into a local studio to record a demo for submission. Once approved, he recorded the finished song and delivered it to the club offices in Melbourne. It sounded awesome, and still sounds awesome to this day. The lyrics that the Brisbane players sing after each win are Jim's and are always sung loud and proud.

Sadly, Flo passed away soon after and I attended her funeral in Thornbury. Colin scattered Flo's ashes under the goal posts of the Brunswick Street Oval, the old home ground of Fitzroy Football Club. One misty, winter's morning, I met Colin walking alone down our street and asked him what he was doing out so early on such a cold day. He told me he'd taken the tram down St Georges Road to visit Flo under the goalposts and watch the sunrise. It was my great privilege to have known Colin and Flo.

*

During maternity leave, I set up a home office and resumed writing, something I had loved since childhood and hadn't done for many years. Rediscovering my passion for words was easy when combined with my love of travel, history and art. To my great delight, my travel articles were accepted for publication and syndicated nationally.

Although I returned to work from maternity leave for a few months, I had already begun setting up the home office to include Jim's business as well as my own. Using my business contacts, we began booking corporate work for Jim, which went so well that it wasn't long before we made the decision that I was needed full time in our family business. Business went from strength to strength with Jim having a professional office behind him for the first time, allowing him to generate income creatively while I handled the day-to-day business aspects.

In 1998, Australia Post released its first Australian Rock'n'Roll stamps. Jim, who had been an avid philatelist all his life, was thrilled to learn that one of his songs would be immortalised on a postage stamp. To him, it was one of the greatest accolades of his life. He was also a great collector of music memorabilia, and he quickly came up with a business idea that combined both of his collecting passions in posters of the stamp artwork framed with a First Day Cover autographed by the artist.

A First Day Cover is a collector's item issued by the post office on the first day of the release of a new stamp. For the Rock'n'Roll stamp issue, the covers were envelopes that were pre-printed with the stamps being released on that day. Australia Post franked the stamps on the envelopes – or date stamped them – with the date of the first day of issue.

With permission from Australia Post to reproduce the stamp artwork on posters, the First Day Covers were to be mounted on the corresponding poster, which was then matted and framed.

It was an inspired pairing and we submitted a business plan to Australia Post, who also thought it was a great concept and agreed to market six different autographed and framed prints through their outlets. Each print was limited to 500, which meant that each artist would sign 500 autographs. That's a lot of signing. Imagine sitting down and writing your signature 500 times in a row!

Logistically, it was a mammoth task. Firstly, Jim had to contact each artist and ascertain their willingness to participate. In the case of the solo performers, this was just one phone call to his old mates Russell Morris, Normie Rowe and Col Joye. For the bands, each member of Masters Apprentices, Billy Thorpe and the Aztecs, and Sherbet was individually contacted.

The individual performers were scattered far and wide so appointments were scheduled with the various artists in each state and Jim went on the road with 3000 First Day Covers, ensuring each one was personally autographed by every single performer. We booked Jim into city hotels in each state and booked time slots for people to come in and sign. In the days prior, we called to confirm the appointments and I'll always remember the legendary Billy Thorpe's colourful response: "Don't worry," Billy said to Jim, "I won't leave you standing, holding your dick in your hand!"

Sure enough, Billy turned up to Jim's Sydney hotel room at the appointed time and happily signed 500 autographs. Some of the performers asked Jim to travel to their homes and Jim took taxis to various locations. Eventually, the day came when all 3000 First Day Covers were autographed. Sample posters were printed and reprinted until we were satisfied with the quality, then the first orders were framed and delivered to Australia Post. It was an ambitious, challenging project and one of which we were both extremely proud. We were flown to Sydney for the Australia Post Rock'n'Roll stamp launch and Holly came with us for the historic occasion, toddling amongst the luminaries of Australian music in her burgundy velvet pinafore.

*

Nineteen ninety-eight was an incredibly exciting year and ten years since Jim and I first met. Not only were Masters Apprentices commemorated with the Turn Up Your Radio postage stamp, the classic band lineup of Burgess/Ford/Keays/Wheatley was inducted into the ARIA Hall of Fame.

Jim, the only band member from its inception in 1965 who was still in the band, wanted Mick Bower, from the short-lived original 1965 lineup, to be included, but ARIA declined. The award was for the classic band lineup, which had the most success and performed the biggest hits, most of which were penned by Jim Keays and Doug Ford. The two lineups were completely different in every way, the only constant being Jim Keays and the name, Masters Apprentices. Nevertheless, Jim was like a dog with a bone and negotiated for a gold ARIA to be created and delivered to Mick

Bower, the band's first songwriter and the man who thought up the band name. Jim just felt it was the right thing to do.

Yet again, we were flown to Sydney for ARIA awards night and put up at the legendary Sebel Townhouse. It was a black-tie affair so I'd booked into a Surry Hills hair salon in advance for a blow wave. Arriving by taxi back at the Sebel, it wasn't until I entered the foyer and went to get my room key that I found my purse missing. I'd had it in the taxi and, to this day, I don't know if I left it there or if it was pick pocketed in the crowd milling out front of the hotel. Either way, time was tight and Jim was already dressed and waiting for me so I was on the phone to the bank, cancelling credit cards whilst doing my makeup, getting dressed and walking to the limo.

It wasn't until I exited the car and stepped onto the red carpet with Jim that I took a deep breath and focused on the occasion. Waiting for us on the red carpet was Dianna O'Neill, one of Australia's most respected publicists. Dianna and I had spoken by phone many times, but this was our first meeting in person and the beginning of an enduring and treasured friendship.

In hindsight, the list of VIPs present at the ARIA awards ceremony that evening can quite rightly be described as legendary. Glenn A Baker inducted Masters Apprentices into the Hall Of Fame and Angry Anderson from Rose Tattoo inducted The Angels. Watching footage of Jim, Glenn Wheatley, Colin Burgess and Doc Neeson, all titans of Australian music who are no longer with us, I still marvel at the sheer volume of talent that was gathered under the same roof. Sitting in the audience, I witnessed former Prime Minister Gough Whitlam's musical namesakes genuflect before him and watched transfixed as Regurgitator, Living End and Natalie Imbruglia electrified the entire auditorium. Archie Roach, Kylie Minogue, The Wiggles, Julian Lennon, Savage Garden, Silverchair and many more, all in the one venue.

After accepting his award and returning to his seat, Jim whispered to me excitedly that he had just met The Wiggles backstage! Given the list of luminaries above, this may sound strange, but Holly was a pre-schooler and The Wiggles videos, with Dorothy the Dinosaur and Captain Feathersword, were on high rotation at our house for many years.

The official after party was held at another venue within walking distance and the route was cordoned off with minders along the way to ensure that nobody got lost after a few champagnes. Jim gave me the gold ARIA to hold while he signed autographs. It was dangerously heavy with a sharp point at the top and so shiny that it seemed a shame to put fingerprints all over it, so I had the bright idea of wrapping it in a linen napkin. As we stepped out into the night air, I adjusted my grip on the ARIA and it slid straight out of the linen cloth, glanced off my foot and clanged into the bluestone gutter. The ARIA fared better than my foot, which was bruised for weeks. That ARIA award is currently on display in the Australian Music Vault in Melbourne and, if you look closely enough, you can still see a slight ding.

The next morning we set the alarm in time to have a long breakfast in bed at The Sebel in celebration of our 9th wedding anniversary before heading back to Melbourne. Nine years of marriage and ten years together was worthy of celebration. We'd weathered the storm of recession and the ensuing income drought together and we were now reaping the benefits of our love, commitment and hard work.

We had a beautiful daughter, a thriving business, a close circle of friends and the means to travel regularly interstate and overseas to visit our extended family. Holly commenced kindergarten and we began to look at schools, which led us to look further afield than the local public schools. Frank and Liz had already moved bayside and our Cardiology nights were less frequent as a result. The house in Thornbury needed major renovation if we were to stay much longer but there seemed little point as we had already started looking at houses in the eastern suburbs. The beautiful, leafy streets and plethora of good schools beckoned.

Our little Thornbury home went on the market and we bought an historic 1920's home in a leafy suburb which, we later learned from an elderly neighbour, had been the old station master's home. It had a wide return verandah on two sides that reminded me of the old Queenslander home in which I'd lived as a child, and a romantic garden that brought beauty, shade and privacy replete with rambling roses, silver birch, Japanese maple and fruit trees. We put a wooden child's seat for two beneath what became known as The Fairy Tree. Holly christened it The Magic Garden and indeed it was. Fragrant, with dappled sunlight on velvety grass and plenty of little 'rooms' in which to play and daydream, it wasn't huge, but it was perfect for us.

There really was a lot happening all at once because while we were busy buying and selling houses, Jim had also been in discussions with Russell Morris and Darryl Cotton about working as a trio. Darryl and Russell had been working very successfully with Ronnie Burns as Burns, Cotton & Morris, but Ronnie had given his notice and Jim's best mate, Russell, was keen to bring Jim into the mix. I'd met Darryl a few times at various gigs with Jim and really liked him.

Three legendary lead singers, contemporaries from the sixties, each a megastar in his own right, now coming together. Russell had always been a solo artist but Darryl and Jim had begun their careers in the sixties as front men for the their bands, Zoot and Masters Apprentices respectively. Both had been pin-up boys for their legions of fans, but that is where the similarities appeared to end. Apparently, Zoot and Masters Apprentices had not been friends in their heyday, with the Masters having a reputation as bad boys in black leather and Zoot wearing their signature pink clothing. Both were managed by the late Darryl Sambell, who also managed Johnny Farnham. Between the two bands though, instead of camaraderie there had been an unfriendly, sometimes spiteful competition and both Jim and Darryl were still wary of each other. When Jim told me this, I looked at him in disbelief.

"How old are you guys?" I asked. I couldn't believe they were still holding grudges from when I was a baby.

It was not long afterwards that Jim came out of the storage room carrying a large, framed poster of Zoot from his collection of memorabilia and I looked at him in bewilderment.

"I was thinking Darryl might appreciate this," said Jim by way of explanation.

I smiled and agreed that Darryl would probably love it and giving it to him would be a nice thing to do. It was the rock'n'roll equivalent of an olive branch, given as a peace offering and accepted in kind.

Before long, rehearsals were booked in, and Jim started learning Darryl Cotton's and Russell's extensive song list. Darryl, Russ and the band only needed to learn Jim's chosen songs, but they also took the opportunity to refresh their set list and rehearse different songs from their impressive catalogues.

It was an exciting time but also a slightly daunting one for Jim. One of the many things I admired about my darling husband was his supreme confidence in his own ability. Jim had never suffered from self-doubt or stage fright, but he confided in me, that for the first time in his life, he worried that he might be out of his league. In Cotton Keays & Morris, Jim would be required to sing intricate harmonies on many of the most famous hits in Australian music. Any mistakes and the audience would be right onto it. His own singing style was a mixture of snarly garage punk and blues-based rock that was not big on harmonies. It was the first time I'd ever heard Jim express the slightest trace of nervousness and my heart went out to him. Typically for Jim, it was only fleeting because he then did what he always did in life and applied himself to learning the songs with a single-minded professionalism and perseverance that saw him achieve whatever he set his mind to.

Over the next 13 years, Cotton Keays & Morris were consistently one of the most successful live music bands in Australia.

"All killer, no filler," as the boys would often say on stage.

Between the three principals, they had a multitude of hits and a plethora of lesser-known album tracks that were audience favourites. They could change up their set list regularly and still leave out a whole swag of really great songs, such was the depth of the song pool at their fingertips. The on-stage banter and anecdotes between the three rock legends quickly developed and evolved to be an integral part of the show that the audience loved, but their off-stage antics were even better.

Life on the road and at home with Cotton Keays & Morris was ridiculously hilarious, sometimes dramatic and always far more entertaining than any 'reality TV' show. If a film producer had shown the foresight to have a camera crew shadow them on the road and at home, Cotton Keays & Morris and their families would have been international superstars. No doubt about it.

## Chapter Four

# The Only Ones

*"The future depends on what we do in the present."*
*~ Mahatma Gandhi*

At the turn of the millennium, we were well and truly settled into our new home and Cotton Keays & Morris continued to go from strength to strength. Our family friendship group had grown to embrace a whole new set of friends outside of the entertainment world with neighbours and families from the kindergartens that Holly attended. The time had come to enrol Holly in the local primary school, and I felt a slight sadness that, as our only child together, she was missing out on the gift of growing up with a sibling.

Jim and I talked about it and decided that we would try for another baby. Jim was happy to grow our family; his only concern was that he would be working and regularly travelling away from home.

"You'll be the one doing all the work," he said.

That didn't bother me at all as I'd happily taken on most of the parental duties anyway. I loved our family life and loved being a wife, mother and business partner. It was a joy and I still had plenty of energy and love to share.

Bonnie was conceived within weeks of my stopping the pill, which was no surprise. A kindergarten mum later said to me, we owe it to ourselves to have a second child because we know what we're doing the second time around. Like it or not, it is the lot of firstborn children to have first-time parents, well-meaning couples who learn as they go. Being a firstborn myself, I remember wondering as a child why my little sister seemed to get away with a lot more than I ever did. Still, my sister is, and always will be, one of the greatest gifts in my life and I wanted that gift for Holly, too. As an only child, it was something that Jim never had.

The midwife-led birth centre where I gave birth to Holly had a 24-hour checkout policy, which appealed to me at the time. The option was available to move to the maternity ward, but the prospect of sharing a ward room with three other mothers, their newborns and visitors did not seem restful. I preferred to be in my own home. I later realised that, as a first-time mum, I'd gone home too soon. Although my own mum had been there for a while, once she went back to the Gold Coast, I was on my own. The public child health care nurse I visited regularly with Holly appeared overworked and underfunded and I was concerned about my care with our next child. One of our neighbours, a mother of four, came over and helped me with getting Holly settled into a regular sleeping pattern. My friend, Nicki, came down to visit from the Gold Coast, allowing me to get the anecdotal help and advice I hadn't known that I needed to get my breastfeeding on track. Nicki was pretty, vivacious and witty. She was also another Sagittarian... surprise, surprise! We had been out on the town together in Surfers Paradise on the night she met and fell in love with her future husband.

I'll never forget the time that I walked into her house while she was having a lively debate with her stepmother in the lead-up to her wedding on the Gold Coast, at which I was to be bridesmaid. They were debating the sex appeal of rockstars and whose era had the best looking men. Nicki was of the opinion that no man of any decade could be better looking than Jon Bon Jovi. Her stepmother, however, was adamant that the rockstars of her youth way surpassed the ones of today. She kept saying there was one guy who was sexier than any man she'd seen before or since but couldn't remember his name. After a while, she said, "I've got it! His name was Jim Keays!"

Nicki thought she was having a joke, until she realised that her stepmother had no idea who I was engaged to marry. Nicki and I couldn't believe that neither of us had heard of Jim until I moved to Melbourne. Needless to say, I was seated at the table with the bridal party and Jim was seated next to his Number One fan!

With the long recovery from Holly's birth in mind, I wanted to do things differently with Bonnie's pregnancy six years later. Although we had no private health insurance, I hoped to return to the public birth centre for a natural, midwife-led birth, then recuperate in the adjoining private hospital as a self-funded patient.

It soon became frustratingly apparent to me that the medical system would not allow this cross-over from public to private. I learned from my experience, that private hospitals would only take patients under the care of a private obstetrician who chose to utilise that private hospital. Private hospital revenue is generated by patients of doctors in private practice who use the facilities. I'd never really thought about it before, but even in 2001, it looked to me like the first loyalty of private hospitals was to the doctors who chose to utilise their facility.

Many years later, I would come to question the ethics of a private system that is propped up with public monies. A system that excludes the majority of taxpayers who contribute to it, because many are unable to afford it, and allows private doctors and corporations to earn lucrative sums of money, in addition to what the doctors earn in the public system (because doctors start off being trained in the public system and many continue to work in both sectors).

Initially, I chose to remain with the public system, but my experience of the birth centre during my early term visits was very different from six years prior. The centre itself looked tired in comparison to my experience there birthing Holly and appeared to be suffering from cutbacks, with a view to its eventual closure. Most worrying to me was how the number of midwives working in the centre appeared to be reduced. As parents, Jim and I wanted the best of care for our baby and in our opinion, we felt this was no longer right for our family.

I went to a GP, who referred me to a private obstetrician who operated out of hospitals in the eastern suburbs. When I called to book an appointment, I was told that he was already fully booked past my due date and wasn't taking on new patients, which was worrying as it looked like I had left it too late to investigate alternatives.

However, one of our neighbours highly recommended a local obstetrician who worked out of the same hospitals and was also their close family friend. Soon enough, I had a new referral, then an appointment with this obstetrician, and I was booked into a nearby private hospital as a self-funded patient.

Around the halfway mark of my pregnancy, I suddenly developed excruciating abdominal pain that did not pass. Jim and I were frightened because although we weren't doctors, we didn't think intense abdominal pain in pregnancy was a good thing. Jim thought it might be early labour pain, but I thought it felt different. Jim called the hospital and he was instructed to bring me in straight away.

My private obstetrician was having time off and his patients were being seen by his covering colleague. An ultrasound was ordered and failed to show any reason for the pain. Thankfully, the baby was fine and regular monitoring continued to confirm that my womb and my baby were perfectly healthy. I was given medication for the mystery pain and sent home.

The pain did not abate and, being the sort of person who gives up drinking tea and coffee whilst pregnant and breastfeeding, taking pain relief medication did not sit well with me. Jim was still worried about my health, so we decided to go to the public hospital where I'd birthed Holly for a second opinion. We presented at emergency and because they were unable to diagnose a reason for the pain, I was admitted to the ward for monitoring.

The public system was slow, clunky but ultimately effective. The ward looked just as tired as the birth centre had. Some days the freshly changed bedsheets were so worn that they had handstitched repairs in them. The cleanliness was questionable, too. I watched cleaners do the floors daily and every day they failed to clean behind the bedside table, missing the old, used dressing that lay there amongst the dust bunnies. I was there for around a week doing little more than going to radiology for daily ultrasounds, as X-rays are not performed on pregnant women. There was a lot of lying around in bed waiting, but at least I was monitored regularly and reassured each time that my baby was healthy.

One day Jim phoned to find me in tears of fear and frustration. I'd realised that the problem was with me, not the baby. The best that they could tell me was that more tests had been ordered, but nothing seemed to be happening. After we spoke, Jim called the hospital. I'm not sure what he said, but within minutes there was a doctor at my bedside. He was not happy and stood over me, pointed his finger at me and lectured me very sternly, telling me that I should not be crying to my husband and to let the doctors do their jobs. I felt trapped and disempowered. Where else was I to go?

After the doctor left, a nurse came to see me and I told her what had occurred. She seemed worried and told me that I should not have been spoken to like that. She asked if I wanted to file a complaint, but I declined. I just wanted to get better and get out of there and felt that making a formal complaint would only inflame the situation.

Nevertheless, Jim's call seemed to get things moving along because the next trip down to radiology for an ultrasound, although exhaustive, was successful. The sonographer spent a very long time examining me, much longer than any previously. She kept zeroing in, looking really closely from every angle until, at last, she exclaimed excitedly that she was going to get her colleagues to have a look at what she'd found. The little space soon filled up with people all marvelling at the screen, which showed a kidney stone that was trapped in my ureter, rattling around in the tube between my kidney and bladder. The cause of all the pain and commotion was 'renal colic', a kidney stone.

Once they had a diagnosis, a urologist came to see me. He told me that kidney stones were usually found with X-ray and notoriously difficult to find with ultrasound. No wonder the sonographers were so excited. There was no safe treatment available to me whilst pregnant so he prescribed some stronger pain relief, telling me to come and see him in his rooms after I'd had the baby. Jim was called and came straight away to pick me up and take me home, to my inexpressible relief. My baby was fine and the pain was manageable and not life-threatening. Having experienced both, I can say unequivocally that the pain of renal colic far exceeds the pain of labour. I'd choose childbirth over kidney stones any day of the week.

At the next antenatal visit with the private obstetrician, he seemed uncomfortable that I had gone to the public hospital for diagnosis, saying he couldn't believe I'd done that. To me, it had seemed like an obvious next step after I'd been sent home from the private hospital without a diagnosis. I told him how the kidney stone had been found and how the radiologists had found it so interesting.

"You don't want to be interesting to *them*, Karin," was his dry response.

It was on the tip of my tongue to reply that thank goodness they *were* interested otherwise I'd be sitting there in front him, still in agony and wondering what was wrong. Swallowing the retort, I said nothing more on the subject and focused on looking forward to the remainder of my pregnancy, which thankfully was mostly smooth sailing.

Keeping up with our family's tradition of birthdays in Virgo, Bonnie was born in September, two weeks over the due date. I quite liked being the only Sagittarian amongst all those Virgos. Jim, himself a Virgo, loved to say that Virgos can be a pain in the arse and need a Saggi to keep them from taking themselves too seriously. In a re-run of Holly's birth, I was booked in to be induced on the morning of Bonnie's birth; however, I somehow avoided this once more. It may have been coincidence, but I did follow the same routine, which included taking a natural laxative before bed the night before.

At midnight, I was awoken by a contraction and my waters broke immediately. I called the hospital and was told to come in for monitoring as it was the obstetrician's policy to monitor babies once the membranes were ruptured. I remember feeling hampered by the cardiotocograph (usually referred to as a CTG for short) as I was unable to walk around while being monitored, but the midwife insisted that I lie back and have the CTG.

Once again, the midwife had no idea of how advanced my labour was, probably because my demeanour gave no indication. She had gone on a break when I recognised the urge to push and called for the midwife to check my dilation. She took one look and told me the baby's head was crowning. I began pushing once the midwife gave the okay and the obstetrician arrived just in time to do an episiotomy. Just like clockwork, the birth was drug-free and Bonnie was born at 3:06 am, healthy and even bigger than Holly at 9 lb 9 oz (4320 g). My second labour was much quicker than my first: a total of 3 hours from the first contraction.

This time around, my post-natal experience was a revelation. I stayed in the hospital for four days and benefitted from the undoubted experience of the midwives, who ensured that I got plenty of rest and that my breastfeeding was well established. The private room soon overflowed with masses of flowers as friends came to visit and meet Bonnie. She was a dream baby who smiled at the midwife on the delivery table, fed like a trooper and slept all night from the day she was born.

Family life resumed when we got home and Bonnie fitted into it seamlessly. She slept all night, every night, and woke up for a feed with a smile on her face before going back to sleep. It was all so easy and so much fun that I wondered why I hadn't done it sooner!

One night, early in 2002, I was drifting off to sleep when the bed started shaking so violently that I thought we were having an earth tremor. It was quite scary and, as I lay there waiting for it to stop, it slowly dawned on me that maybe it wasn't the bed that was shaking. It was me. My chest was pounding so hard that it felt like the whole bed was jumping up and down and I could scarcely catch my breath.

When it subsided, I went out to the lounge room to find Jim. Ridiculous as it may sound, I did ask my husband if he felt the earth move even though we were at opposite ends of the house! Jokes aside, I had a terrible headache and felt sick so we agreed that I should make a time to see the GP the next day.

Murphy's Law prevailed and the GP found nothing amiss. My heart was beating normally so she wrote me a referral and told me to go straight to the local pathology lab for an ECG if it happened again. Little did I know at the time, but I was soon to have my first experience of medical error as a result.

I began to notice that from time to time my heart would do a strange little racing thing and then jump... sort of stopping... which made me lightheaded. It seemed to be worse in the shower. Everything went grey when I took a shower and it was difficult to breathe. At first, it would only be for a few seconds, then nothing for ages, but it gradually became more frequent until one morning it started and didn't stop. I had almost passed out, crawling on the floor because I couldn't stand up and that was how Jim found me. He bundled me into the car and raced me to a pathology lab that was just down the street.

Time was of the essence. We handed them the GP's referral and I was taken straight in and hooked up to their ECG monitor. What bothered me most was the look on the technician's face when the trace began. She looked very, very worried. In fact, she looked downright grim. Then, just like that, it stopped. My heart was back to normal, although I was left feeling sick and exhausted.

The technician explained that due to the urgency of the situation and the need to catch whatever it was that my heart was doing, she had applied the electrodes to my chest and body and started the trace without first keying my name and details into the machine. This turned out to be the correct decision on the part of the technician because, due to her swift action, she had captured an electronic trace of whatever my heart was doing.

However, that trace of my heart actually had another woman's details on it, a woman who had been in just before me. I vaguely recalled passing a young woman on her way out as I came in and assumed it was her. The technician explained the situation to me very clearly and wrote a detailed explanation on the trace for the doctor to whom it would be sent for analysis.

She then entered my details into the machine and started a second trace. We spent the best part of an hour trying to get my heart to misbehave again. I stood up and paced back and forth, then ran on the spot. I touched my toes and did star jumps, but no matter how hard I tried, my heart remained steady. Eventually, we admitted defeat and Jim took me back home but not before the technician reiterated that I must see my doctor as soon as possible for the results of the first ECG.

So when the GP told me a few days later that everything was normal according to the ECG, I was having none of it. Silently blessing the pathology technician for explaining everything to me so clearly, I told the doctor what had occurred.

The GP picked up the phone and spoke with the lab to query the report. When he put the phone down, I knew it wasn't going to be good; he had the appearance of one who was trying to remain calm in the face of alarming news.

My heart had developed an arrhythmia, he said. A particularly dangerous kind, called ventricular tachycardia (or VT), that caused my heart to beat at an abnormally high rate.

"And what happens then?" I asked.

"It can cause cardiac arrest," he answered.

Even as he spoke, the GP was lifting the telephone handset to his ear and calling a cardiologist for an emergency appointment.

Later on, I would wonder what had happened to the woman whose name was on the first part of my ECG. Had she been diagnosed with a life-threatening condition that she never actually had?

The news only got worse from there, from my perspective anyway. The cardiologist's priority was stopping the arrhythmia and, in his opinion, the best way of doing this was with a particular drug. However, in order to take it, I would have to stop breastfeeding immediately. Bonnie was only five months old and totally breastfed. I was completely unprepared and unwilling to just stop breastfeeding. Bonnie was thriving and my supply was plentiful. So, the cardiologist agreed to start me on a type of drug called 'beta blockers' which would allow me to continue feeding Bonnie. He warned me, though, that if it didn't hold the arrhythmia, I would have to go onto his first choice of medication. It wasn't ideal. I wasn't even drinking tea or coffee whilst breastfeeding so the prospect of taking drugs was anathema to me. However, I reasoned that I at least had time to wean Bonnie onto formula and get her started on solids.

The beta blockers didn't work. The arrhythmia continued and I was told there was no other choice than to begin taking the stronger drug immediately. Bonnie was never to be breastfed again. It's called abrupt-weaning, a cruel and traumatic experience for both baby and mother. Jim had been abrupt-weaned at six months of age, when he was given up for adoption, and was so traumatised by the sudden and complete loss of everything he'd ever known and loved that he didn't start speaking until he was five years old.

Frankly, if it wasn't for the dire threat of cardiac arrest, I would have been prepared to live with the symptoms for another month or two, but I was given no choice. One way or another, Bonnie was going to be abrupt-weaned and far better it happened with her mother still alive.

The new drug had such an extensive list of side-effects – over several pages long – that the pharmacist felt compelled to print it out and give it to me when I filled the prescription. So toxic was the treatment that it might well kill me before the heart condition did.

At only five-months, Bonnie could not understand why I would not feed her.

Hours and hours of refusal to take the bottle from Jim was taking its toll on us all. I was in tears, Bonnie was beside herself and Jim was frazzled.

In the end, Kath, our wonderful friend and neighbour, came to the house after answering my distressed call and calmly took Bonnie from Jim, telling me to go for a walk up to the local cafés and have something to eat.

The drug was already affecting me. I could hardly keep my balance and my eyesight was blurred. All this trauma and I still felt every bit as ill and debilitated as I had before the treatment. A call to the cardiologist elicited the curt reply that I must continue to take the medication, probably for the rest of my life. I was devasted because from what I had read in the drug information sheet, that life could well be shortened considerably!

Sitting in that cafe, thinking things through, trying desperately to find a way out of the life mapped out for me by circumstances seemingly beyond my control, I was filled with despair. I was also in shock. Everything had happened too fast to keep up. The life of a woman, a mother, with a chronic heart condition... how could that be mine?

When I got home, things were not much better. We are all born with innate character and personality and Bonnie is one of the most determined personalities I know. Determined to the point of stubborn. The poor little baby, who had hardly let out a single cry in her tiny little life, who had done everything right and fed and slept and smiled like an angel, wanted her mummy and that was that. She didn't know what to do with a bottle, nor did she want to learn, so she cried and refused and wore herself out until she fell asleep hungry. My heart was broken in every way possible.

I went to the other end of the house and cried, too. Eventually, Bonnie did take the bottle and after a few days she stopped trying to find my breast when I fed her and quite happily accepted the bottle from then on. Although I was relieved that Bonnie was happy and settled, the sadness and loss I felt at the abrupt wean was like grief. My painfully engorged breasts reminded me several times a day when my milk let down in readiness to feed my baby.

Not long after, I had a call from Kelly Ford who, after our first meeting whilst I was pregnant with Holly, had become a close family friend. Our daughters, Holly and Leah, are like two peas in a pod. They share the same whacky sense of humour and they look so alike that people assume they are sisters. Each Christmas, when Kelly and I took the girls for Santa photos together, Santa's helpers would often assume that Holly and Leah, both fair-haired with blue eyes, belonged to Kelly and that Bonnie, who is brunette, was mine!

Kelly had just called to say hi and knew nothing of what had occurred in recent weeks, but as I brought her up to date, she had an idea. Kelly told me about a medical specialist who she thought might be of help. Not just any specialist but an electro cardiologist! I had never heard of such a thing but what I had learned from having VT is that the heart has an electrical current. In lay terms, as I understood it, the electrical current of my heart had gone haywire and it was misfiring, causing the VT.

To this day, that electro cardiologist, remains a leading expert in a procedure called radiofrequency ablation. In 2002, he was operating on public patients out of a major hospital and he successfully treated my VT with a same-day procedure! Not even an overnight stay. The VT stopped as a result. Done and dusted, never to return and no more drugs required.

I couldn't understand why I was not told this by my GP. Or the first cardiologist. As a breastfeeding mother, I could not understand why was I not given the option of having the procedure instead of being told my only choices were to take the drug treatment or risk cardiac arrest.

In Australia, with our taxpayer-funded medical system, I naively expected that the doctors who live off our hard-earned taxes would always provide us with the best treatments available. This episode demonstrated to me that my expectations were not being met. Increasingly, I felt that our medical system was run like a corporation, creating an ongoing income stream for doctors by creating patients. It seemed more about keeping pharmaceuticals as the preferred treatment as long as possible. I wasn't sure how else to explain what happened to me.

## Chapter Five

## The Boy from the Stars

*"Without music, life would be a mistake."*
*~ Friedrich Nietzsche*

It was February of 2003 and the Bigger-than-Ben-Hur juggernaut that was the Long Way to the Top concert was about to hit the road for the second tour within twelve months. This regional tour was to be a scaled-down version of the first epic stadium tour.

Billy Thorpe came up with the idea after watching the ABC TV series of the same name. Long Way to the Top (LWTTT) was a national tour of stadium concerts featuring artists from the fifties, sixties and seventies.

The task was Herculean. Twenty-five acts – some of them bands, some individuals – performed their hits live in an epic show, selling out venues around Australia. Audiences came out in their droves to see Australia's rock'n'roll royalty come out to play, one after the other after the other.

The cast read like a who's who of music legends, and Masters Apprentices was among them. Jim reformed the most famous lineup of Keays, Wheatley, Burgess and Ford – although the Wheatley part was flexible. Depending on Glenn's availability, it was either him or his son, Tim, on bass. They were heady days for the cast, many of whom had not performed to such crowds in decades. Jim had been working regularly with Russell Morris and Darryl Cotton as Cotton Keays & Morris for years and was used to pulling crowds at their shows but nothing like the buzz of performing in front of thousands at Rod Laver Arena in Melbourne.

The original tour, including Brian Cadd, was in Brisbane in September 2002. Although I hadn't heard of Jim before moving to Melbourne, I sure knew of Brian Cadd. My parents loved his hit song, 'Little Ray of Sunshine'. I had watched Brian perform 'Moonlight and Roses' on Countdown. What I never knew until I met Jim, was that Brian Cadd had actually written a hit song for Masters Apprentices in the sixties. He called it 'Silver People' but the Masters would release it as 'Elevator Driver'. At the time of writing it, Brian was going by the pseudonym of Brian Caine. A piece of Australian music magic.

Anyway, with the help of Brian Cadd's partner at the time, Linda, we had organised a surprise birthday party for Jim at a bar in the city. The whole cast knew what was going on and I didn't hold out much hope of it staying a secret from Jim, but performers are performers and, when the day came, he had no idea that his family had flown into Brisbane ahead of the whole entourage.

It's funny that people often assume that this would be a common occurrence for high profile performers and their families, just part of the lifestyle. The truth is that I don't know of many partners and families who regularly go out on the road with a band. Any parent knows that travelling with kids requires patience and organisation, and the amount and necessity of those virtues multiplies exponentially when you figure a working rock star into the equation. From a band's perspective, the sometimes-delicate balance of personalities and on-the-road rituals can be thrown off kilter. In the case of LWTTT, though, the whole show was just so darn big that the performers weren't living in each other's pockets, and I knew that our being there would make no difference to anyone other than Jim. So, from my perspective, it wasn't a decision made lightly but definitely one worth the effort on this occasion.

I had organised for our room to be interconnecting with Jim's and we settled ourselves in to wait. The Sheraton's concierge called to let me know when Jim was on his way up to his room and the girls and I sat quietly listening and stifling giggles. Hearing him enter the room next door, I picked up the phone and dialled his room. Of course, he thought I was in Melbourne. I asked him if he could see the birthday present I'd sent in the room.

"No," he said, "I can't see anything here. Maybe they'll bring it up later."

Holly was spluttering behind her hands, which were clapped over her mouth, trying desperately not to giggle out loud.

"It must be there," I said, "I checked with reception before they put me through and they told me it was definitely in your room."

By this time, I couldn't help it, my voice was sounding slightly strangled with the effort of holding back laughter and the girls rolling around on the bed with pillows over their faces weren't helping any.

"Is there a cupboard or something? Check in there."

Jim was starting to sound disappointed after checking the cupboard and finding nothing in the way of birthday pressies and was talking about calling reception to sort it out, so I judged it time to put him out of his misery.

"Can you see another door?" I asked.

"Yes," said Jim, "there's another door but it will go to the next room."

"Well, try it before you call," I said. "Just in case."

Through the phone, I could hear Jim walk over to the door and watched as the door handle turned and the door swung open.

"Happy Birthday, Daddy!" the girls chorused.

The look on Jim's face was priceless, completely delighted and dumbfounded – this was the perfect surprise birthday present. He had been feeling a little unloved because apparently everyone on the bus had been very low-key about his birthday. Earlier in the tour, a birthday cake with sparklers had been produced for someone else but not for him.

So happy was he to see us that we almost couldn't get him out of the room that evening for the birthday dinner I told him I'd booked – he wanted to stay in with us and order room service.

The restaurant was also a bar with a dance floor and music – a perfect choice – and for the second time that day the look on Jim's face was one of utter disbelief and delight.

There they were, a cast of music legends and their entourage, waiting for him around the bar, ready to celebrate… and the party was on.

As one would expect, with that many rock stars in close proximity over so many weeks, the antics behind the scenes rivalled the stage performances for sheer entertainment value. Overall, the feeling amongst the artists was one of mutual respect and the camaraderie was magnified by the sheer number of people on tour together.

*

Rock legends are great to see doing their thing on stage, but they can be more than a little tedious to have around the house when a high-profile tour finishes. All those weeks of being tour-managed and not having to lift a finger for themselves, of having their ego constantly massaged, often means a very different person walks in the front door from the one who left. It's like they need to be house-trained all over again.

Personally, I always found a bag of garbage was the perfect grounding tool when faced with returned rock star attitude. I'd simply empty the kitchen bin and hand the neatly tied bag to Jim with a smile, saying how good it was to have him back so I didn't have to do everything myself. Sometimes he sighed or gave me a blank look, but he usually just took the bag of garbage from my hand and walked out the front door and around the side of the house to where the bins were kept. On the way back, he'd settle into the white wicker lounge on the front verandah, a birthday present he'd bought for me, with the antique brass ashtray that I'd given him early in our marriage. Day or night, there he would sit having a quiet smoke, letting the peace and beauty of our garden weave its grounding magic, bringing him back to himself and the heart and soul of our homelife that he so loved. Without fail, when he walked back in the door a little while later, the abrasive rock star had disappeared and there was my darling once again with his smiling eyes and big, warm hugs.

Rock-star re-education aside, life was good for our family. The leafy suburb of Melbourne in which we lived was a fantastic area to raise a family. The local shopping strip had a village atmosphere and there was no such thing as a quick trip to the shops because there was always at least one person we knew, usually several, shopping there and ready for a chat at any given time.

Holly was in Year 1 at the local school, which was within walking distance of our home, as was the local kinder. Our street and the streets around ours were filled with families and it was the sort of place where everyone knows everyone else and their kids. Christmas drinks at our place in mid-December 2002 saw the house filled with over 100 friends, neighbours and musician-types spilling out into the garden or kicking back on the verandah. The Christmas decorations were up, lights twinkling. By 7:00 pm, the lounge room looked like Santa had already been with masses of brightly wrapped gifts piled beneath the Christmas tree. It seemed as though everyone who walked in the front door left something under the tree on the way through to the kitchen. A magician / face-painter had the kids lining up for his fantasy artwork, later roaming amongst the adults, the sounds of delighted exclamations and laughter ringing out as he confounded them with his magic.

It's funny how some things just stick in your memory... like Bonnie, cute as a button in a yellow and white gingham dress toddling around the food table outside, standing on tiptoe to reach the strawberries on the enormous fruit platter that one of our neighbours had brought. Kids played an impromptu game of cricket in the street; some boys produced water pistols from somewhere, girls squealed and the chase was on. I remember leaning on the verandah rail with Stuart, a school dad and family friend, belting out the Brisbane Lions club song into the night. This was in the days of the legendary Lions three-peat. It was a magical, warm summer's evening and, as our friend, breakfast radio star Peter Stubbs, said as we chatted, nights like this created childhood memories that will stay with the kids for a lifetime.

It was the last Christmas party we ever had.

When I look back to that time, I think of it as the end of the age of innocence for our family. Jim and I had much to be thankful for and we knew it. In thirteen years of marriage, we had faced together our share of life's hardships and challenges. We had worked together to be in the position we now found ourselves – with two beautiful, healthy daughters, a comfortable home filled with a whole lot of love – and we did not take our good fortune for granted.

Christmas came and went and the second half of January saw Jim rehearsing for the regional Long Way to the Top tour. This tour was not the five-star type of tour that the stadium one had been, but it was still a sell-out and definitely worth doing.

For me, it was a time of acceptance and coming to peace with the fact that we would not be having another child. Almost from the day Bonnie was born, I had yearned for a third child. That most mysterious of natural phenomena, the maternal instinct to procreate, decided to kick in at that stage of my life in a major way. Jim and I had talked about it, but he felt that he was getting too old now to become a dad again, especially if we had a boy. He worried that he wouldn't be up for kicking the footy around or playing cricket in ten years' time if we had a son.

Jim was 55 years old when Bonnie was born and looked like a man in his 40s. By anyone's standards, far removed from the typical man of that age... still gigging around the country, fit and healthy with a head full of hair and an irreverent attitude.

No matter his age he was always just Dad to the kids… and he was a good one. Relaxed, fun, loving and reliable, happily married to their mother – not something to be dismissed lightly.

Bonnie had been the easiest, most sweet-natured baby and I felt much more at ease with motherhood second time around. I knew now what I was doing and was more relaxed because I'd done it all before. Plus, I knew now that my body was just made to have babies. It seemed I only had to think that I might like to have a baby et voilà! Well, with a little help from Jim…

\*

Pregnancy suits me. I feel great when I'm pregnant. Since childhood, I had struggled intermittently with low iron. With pregnancy and the cessation of menstruation, I felt alive and energised.

When I was pregnant with Holly, like any first-time mum, the birth experience loomed large. It is normal for first-time mothers to worry about how they will cope. From my own experience of giving birth naturally to Holly and Bonnie, I learned that if mother and baby are both healthy, then natural birth is as much a matter of the mother's state of mind as the body. I had no reason to doubt the wellbeing of my babies and was confident of my own body's ability to give birth so I approached each labour with a sense of anticipation and empowerment.

The feeling that there was another soul waiting to come to Earth through me was strong and I longed for another baby to love and hold. We had so much to give and I was sure in my heart that we would have a son. My sister and I had grown up close to our three cousins – all girls – who were the daughters of our dad's brother. Up to this point, we had produced six granddaughters between us. Not one boy in two generations and it had become something of a running joke in the family each time one of us fell pregnant. My mother must have been convinced that Bonnie was to be a boy because when a box of newborn gifts arrived from Queensland, the clothes were red and blue and the quilt she had stitched herself for the cot was clearly for a boy's room.

I had not been using contraception since Bonnie's birth, but we had not been actively trying to conceive, either, and Jim had taken on responsibility for contraception. I had come to accept that Jim was not sure if he wanted to have another child and, for me, we had to both be sure. So, when Jim left for the regional tour, it seemed to me the perfect window of time to resume the contraceptive pill. The yearning for another baby was still there, but Jim's diary for 2003 was already filling up fast. With a business to run, and two young children to raise, I was at peace with my decision.

So away Jim, Russell and the Long Way to the Top team went, kicking off in Tasmania. The plan was that they would go to NSW from there, until I got a call from Jim saying he and Russell would be coming back to Melbourne for a couple of days and meet up with the rest of the tour in Albury. There were a couple of lay days in the itinerary and they wanted to be home in their own beds rather than hanging around in some hotel unnecessarily.

Jim came home grateful for the chance to be back with our family in our comfortable home so unexpectedly. The regional tour did not have the budget of the original stadium tour and the country motels and gigs were not on the same level, either. Still, Jim must have been feeling energised from the Tassie gigs and came home determined to make the most of it. The first time we made love, I looked across at Jim afterwards and smiled, teasing him about not using contraception.

Jim grinned back and said, "We might have a baby!"

For the next two days, Jim used no contraception. We both knew that there would be no more trying for babies after this. We made love joyously, almost daring the Universe to create another life in this short, unexpected interlude.

For the second time, the girls and I farewelled Jim off on tour and I waited with hope in my heart. My body, always quick to show signs of pregnancy, felt pregnant and I hugged the feeling close. So, when my period arrived some days later, my hopes were dashed and I had to accept that the feelings were nothing more than wishful thinking on my part. The contraceptive pills were in the cupboard and I commenced on Day 1 of the pack. The bleeding stopped quickly and life went on as normal, except that I was still tired and my pelvis was uncomfortable in the way of early pregnancy. I did a couple of pregnancy tests, just to be sure, but they were both negative.

Around ten days later, my breasts started feeling tender. It really felt like I was pregnant, but common sense told me I couldn't be. There was one last pregnancy test left so I decided to use it and put any thought of pregnancy to rest, once and for all. Logic was telling me no even as the test lit up positive immediately and my heart overflowed with joy. I was pregnant! I wanted to tell Jim but he did not have a mobile phone, by choice. He liked the freedom of not being enslaved to a telephone. When on the road, he would call me whenever he arrived at the accommodation and I would pass on any messages and discuss anything that needed his input. This news could not wait so I called Russell Morris. Those two were never far from each other. Russell answered and I knew I'd have to be careful not to give anything away. Russell is as sharp as a tack and it was unusual for me to call him wanting to speak with Jim.

The tour bus had pulled in for a break and Jim was in the service station getting some food. Russell wanted to know if I was okay and he wasn't buying my casual request for Jim to call me back. Russ started giving me the third degree.

"What's happening?" he asked. "You've bought another house?"

"No," I laughed. "Just get him to call me."

"I know something's up," Russell was like a terrier. "You're pregnant?"

"Russell!!" I tried to sound amused and rushed him off the phone. "Just get him to call me, okay?"

The phone rang a few minutes later with Jim sounding worried. "Hi Darl, are you okay?"

"Yes, I'm great! I have some news for you. Are you sitting down?"

"Yes," he said, still sounding concerned. "I'm on the bus. What is it?"

"I'm pregnant!" I just said it straight out and waited. Word for word, this is how it went. If only there'd been a film crew on hand!

"No!" Jim sounded faint.

"Yes!" I replied.

"NO!" Jim sounded more adamant, and I started to worry that he might not be happy about the news.

"YES!" By this time, I was almost yelling and was about to ask him if he had any problem with that. Later, I learned that the whole bus was hanging on his next words, wondering what could possibly be going on.

Then Jim yelled out to the entire bus, "I'm going to be a Daddy! We're having a baby!"

From somewhere far away in rural Australia, I could hear uproarious cheering and whooping congratulations. Col Joye produced a bottle of Scotch from his luggage and the cast and entourage proceeded to toast the news of our new baby, the only baby conceived by a cast member on the legendary Long Way to the Top tour.

## Chapter Six

# Waiting for the Big One

*"It's easy to scare women. It's even profitable to scare women... but it's not nice, so let's stop it."*
*~ Ina May Gaskin, midwife and author of*
Spiritual Midwifery

There can a subtle shift in the attitude of some people towards mothers who have more than two children. It's sort of a "you made your own bed so now lie in it" feeling – hard to put a finger on and often coming from unexpected quarters. Certainly, I felt that I had to keep the family's day-to-day life going and not let Jim or the girls be disadvantaged by the new family member's imminent arrival.

Four days out from my due date, I had the steam cleaners through the house in the morning, shopped for groceries and collected the doonas from the drycleaner, then drove out to the airport to pick up my Aunt Valerie who had flown from the Gold Coast to help me out in the final days of the pregnancy and to look after the girls while I was in hospital. Far more to me than a beloved aunt, Valerie was my treasured friend and mentor, herself a mother of four.

Jim's touring schedule was solid that whole year and he was working interstate right throughout September and October of 2003. For Cotton Keays & Morris, this typically meant flying out on Thursday morning and returning Monday afternoon. On this particular day, though, he was in bed all day trying to recover from a virus before the flight to Adelaide the next day.

At age 38, I was too old for the family birth centre and besides, I'd come to trust the obstetrician as I believed he respected my views in allowing Bonnie to go further overdue. During that pregnancy with Bonnie, I suffered more physical discomfort than I ever did when pregnant with William.

It was some weeks prior to my due date that the obstetrician had first raised the potential of induction at one of my antenatal appointments. His actual words were, "I won't let you go two weeks over this time, Karin." I questioned him as to why and he said because William was a big baby, and a boy, and he was worried about shoulder dystocia. He also mentioned my age and the potential for problems with the placenta.

I went home and told Jim what the obstetrician had said. We were both unconvinced that induction was necessary as there was no actual problem with William. Jim asked questions that I was unable to answer so we agreed that he would come with me to a future appointment to discuss it. On our wedding anniversary, Jim and I sat in the obstetrician's office and questioned him on the need to induce. Of most concern to me was the mention of the possible complication of shoulder dystocia. According to the obstetrician, it was a birth injury more common in boys as they have wider shoulders. He said that William was a big baby, bigger than the girls. When shoulder dystocia occurs, the baby's shoulders get stuck inside the pelvis during labour. In his words, once the head is through the cervix, you're committed. As I understood it, should William's shoulders become stuck once his head was in the birth canal, caesarean was not an option. That was all he said, but it sounded horrific to me. I imagined my baby's bones being broken, or worse.

Years on, when I discovered the inspirational and tireless work of renowned midwife Ina May Gaskin, author of *Spiritual Midwifery*, I learned that the simple act of assisting the mother into a kneeling position on all fours means the rotation is often enough to free the shoulders of babies experiencing shoulder dystocia. This is now known in obstetrics as the Gaskin Manoeuver. In my opinion, introducing the possibility of shoulder dystocia to any pregnant woman is guaranteed to create a sense of fear for her baby's wellbeing. I certainly felt that fear.

The reading list for pregnant mothers provided by the obstetrician and hospital did not contain *Spiritual Midwifery*. The books that they recommended, and which I dutifully bought and referred to throughout all my pregnancies, all said the same thing about induction. In essence, their message was to trust in the medical professionals and follow their instructions as they would only intervene if it was in the best interests of mother and baby.

William's due date of Monday, 27 October came and went. There was no sign of impending labour, but that did not surprise me. My body just carries my babies longer. I felt that William wasn't ready to leave the womb. He wasn't cooked yet.

The obstetrician had told me to make an appointment time to see him on Friday, 31 October, whereupon he would book me in for induction, saying he felt "this baby needs to come out sooner rather than later." Friday, 31 October was Halloween. I didn't know much about Halloween, but I did know that being four days over my due date was way too early for my body to give birth and thought that I'd be able to put off being induced for another few days, at least. I reasoned that I probably had until Wednesday, given the configuration of a weekend, followed by the Melbourne Cup public holiday on Tuesday. That would make it ten days past the due date, early by my body's standards, but I felt okay with the compromise, given the obstetrician's opinion.

To be honest, I really didn't think it would get to the stage where I would have to be induced. Twice in the past, I had managed to escape the dreaded drip at the last moment and I had no reason to think this time would be any different. I knew what to do to get things going and had, in my mind, enough time to do it.

A phone call to his receptionist on the Thursday, one day before Halloween, left me slightly uneasy. The obstetrician would see me tomorrow at 10:00 am in his rooms adjoining the hospital. I had never seen him there before. I had only ever seen him at his Clayton rooms – I didn't even know he had rooms at the hospital.

Had this been happening today, I would have long ago Googled all the information I needed from both medical and non-interventionist perspectives. It seems unbelievable now but, in 2003 we had to dial up internet on a big, boxy computer, which could take an hour to load. Not that there was much to find in relation to being induced – not how they did it or what drugs they used, anyway. The internet back then was not filled with the amount of information that is now available at our fingertips.

All I remembered was what the midwife had said when I was pregnant with Holly about how Syntocinon, the drug used to induce labour via a drip, made labour more painful. That was 1995 and Holly was eleven days overdue. In 2001, Bonnie was two weeks overdue. By that time, it was obvious that the girls needed to come out to avoid potential complications, so I never really felt that I needed to research it. I'm not sure how and where I could have done that back then, anyway.

With induction a very real possibility, I researched this drug as best I could on the internet. Had this been happening today, I would have found numerous references to foetal distress during artificial induction of labour but, in 2003 I didn't find much information regarding its use.

Having gleaned as much information as I could find on Syntocinon, I ran a search on Halloween. Ironically, that search returned a lot more information. I soon learned that Halloween is an abbreviated version of 'Hallowed Evening' and that it is the day leading into All Hallows Day, which is also called Samhain. All Hallows Day is the Christian name for the ancient Celtic festival of Samhain, a period of 24 hours where the veil between the spiritual and physical world is believed to thin, allowing the souls of dead kin to visit their family.

Jim was working in Sydney and wasn't due to fly into Melbourne until 2:00 pm on the Friday. So that sealed it. Unless I went into labour naturally, no way was my baby being born on Halloween, or on that Friday, whether it was Halloween or not. Besides, I still felt it was far too early. The more time he spent in the safe, nourishing environment of my womb, the better. The obstetrician's reasons for induction had centred on William's apparently large size and, to a lesser degree, my age. I wasn't convinced the age factor was relevant; it was just a statistic. Doctors routinely use statistics to justify their actions and decisions, so I put no faith in that one. As any high school math student or sales representative will attest, all data can be manipulated to support a desired outcome.

So it was that I drove to the hospital on Halloween with Bonnie and my Auntie Valerie for support. The waiting room had the obligatory toy box for children, and I left Bonnie playing happily alongside Valerie when I was called in to see the obstetrician. He looked tired and slightly dishevelled, which was unusual for him but only to be expected for someone whose work involved being called out to attend births at all hours of the day and night.

Lying on the table, I braced myself for a cervical exam to determine the ripeness of my cervix. The softer it is, the more fingers the obstetrician or midwife can fit into the opening as the cervix prepares itself to stretch the 10 cm required for a baby's head to fit through. Giving the membrane 'a bit of a tickle' is thought to help get things going. I'd had the same exam with Holly and Bonnie and neither had been a pleasant experience. However, this time I actually winced. It hurt so much that my eyes smarted with tears.

As I surreptitiously brushed away the tears, the obstetrician disposed of the gloves he'd used and told me over his shoulder as he washed his hands that my cervix was 1–2 cm dilated and William's head was well down. This meant that my baby's head was 'engaged' in the bony part of my pelvis in preparation for birth. I had already felt that myself.

The whole natural birth process is such a miracle of nature. Somehow babies know, at a certain point in time, to fit the top of their heads into that cradle of their mother's bones in readiness for birth. They stop trying to turn around and do all the acrobatics of the previous months and they become quieter. Waiting. For the mother, the breathlessness caused by the baby pushing against her ribs eases and is replaced by a feeling of heaviness in the pelvis and constant pressure on the bladder.

Although I knew William's head was engaged, the thought occurred to me that it felt as though the obstetrician really had to force his fingers in the cervical opening and maybe it wasn't as soft, and therefore ripe, as it should be.

The obstetrician's next words jolted me. He felt that rupturing the membranes should be enough to get labour started and he would book me into hospital to be induced later that day.

My expectation of a natural birth was looking more unrealistic by the minute, but I flatly refused to be induced that day, explaining about Jim's flight schedule and saying firmly that I would not go ahead without him. I didn't mention my fears of a Halloween birth, very aware of how it might sound.

Plus, I had yet to try taking the dose of the same natural laxative that I believed had brought on labour with both of the girls, thereby avoiding induction. He seemed irritated and told me not to take it because "it doesn't work", to which I replied that *it only works if the baby is ready to come*.

His reply was that it would have to be done tomorrow. He told me that he would go to the gym in the morning and that I should be at the hospital at 8:30 am for a 9:00 am start.

As I drove home with Valerie and Bonnie, I couldn't help but feel uneasy, that this was not right. The feeling of the cervical examination was different. I hadn't considered that he would induce me on a Saturday. I don't know why, but I hadn't. Saturday was also Samhain, the day *after* Halloween. If my aversion to my baby being induced on Halloween was a consideration, then that aversion went into overdrive at the prospect of it being done on Samhain.

Later on, long after the day of William's birth, my friend Sherrin quietly commented that nothing about that day was right. We arrived home from the appointment with the obstetrician and I was on edge awaiting Jim's return so I could fill him in and discuss what we should do. If the natural laxative did not work, I was reluctant to be induced the next day. My maternal instinct and previous birth experience told me it was too soon. On the other hand, going against the professional opinion of a doctor we trusted and had employed to ensure the wellbeing of our baby was a massive call. What if I delayed and something happened to William in the meantime? I needed to speak with Jim.

When Jim finally walked through the door later that afternoon, it was a huge relief to see him. Caught up in the girls' excitement of his arrival home, we didn't get much time to talk privately about my appointment with the obstetrician that afternoon. Fully discussing the heaviness on my mind had to wait until later that evening. Just as I had done on the night before Holly's and Bonnie's births, we went for a walk. Jim picked up take-away dinner from our favourite Indian restaurant, Tandoori Den. Instead of my usual butter chicken, it was vindaloo for me: the hotter, the better to get things moving, I thought. After dinner, I finished packing my bag for hospital before showering and taking the natural laxative in orange juice. All was in readiness. Jim and I had finally found time to talk, and we were both on the same page. All we had ever wanted is for our children to be healthy and happy. Was being induced the way to ensure William's health? Neither of us were keen on medical intervention, but we both agreed that we did not have enough medical knowledge to go against the advice of the obstetrician we had employed to ensure the wellbeing of William and myself. Moreover, he had been quite hands-off with Bonnie's birth, allowing it to go two weeks past her due date, which we were happy with. We both fervently hoped that my usual night-before-induction routine would do the trick. If not, we agreed that we would leave for the hospital at 8.00 am the next morning.

Meanwhile, Valerie had received a worrying phone call from home on the Gold Coast. Her husband, my uncle Maurie, had taken a turn whilst in the pool. He was swimming underwater and became disorientated and had almost drowned. Valerie needed to go home. We managed to book a flight for the Saturday and Sherrin would pick up Valerie from our house and take her to the airport. This now meant that there would be nobody at home with the girls and I asked our friend and neighbour, Lisa, if she would look after them.

That night, my pre-birth routine created the familiar purge, but it failed to bring on labour. I tried my best to get some sleep but lay awake worrying that my baby was not ready to be born. Jim and I had discussed it in depth, long into the evening, and we both had strong doubts about the necessity to induce. At times, the discussion verged on slightly fraught. My reservations were based on my two previous birth experiences, on knowledge of and trust in my own body. After all, Holly's and Bonnie's births were way more overdue than this one was going to be. Whilst agreeing with me on this, Jim was also mindful of upcoming gigs, unable to be in two places at once.

He expressed his frustration at the lack of certainty, saying, "Well, when *is* this baby going to be born?"

My answer was, of course, when he's ready.

In the end, though, our concern for William's wellbeing was paramount and we felt that we had to trust the obstetrician's professional advice. The fact that he allowed Bonnie to go two weeks overdue made us feel that we could trust his judgement.

Sometime during the night, I had what I can only describe as a premonition. It was an overwhelming feeling of impending doom, a knowledge that something truly terrible would happen if I allowed William to be induced the next day. I knew with absolute certainty that I could not allow it and decided to call the obstetrician at the earliest opportunity. I watched the clock throughout the night and left a message with his call service at 6:30 am. When he called, it was apparent that the call had woken him up.

Me: Hello.

Him: It's ---. [obviously been woken up]

Me: Sorry to call you so early. I took the natural laxative and have had no contractions. I've decided that I don't want to be induced today. I don't have a good feeling about it. Can we please do it tomorrow?

Him: [sounding annoyed] I can't do it tomorrow, Karen (sic.), I've made commitments to my family for the next three days. I have my Leongatha practice on Wednesday and I won't be back until Thursday. I feel that's too long to wait.

Me: [probably sounding fairly mutinous, as I had just found out that he was working around a personal schedule] I just don't want to do it today.

Him: [obviously trying to sound patient] I guess I'm trying to understand why you are so adamant about not doing it today?

Me: I have a really bad feeling about doing it today. I feel as though I am being pushed into doing something that I don't want to do to suit other people's schedules.

Him: [very reluctantly] Well, you could be induced by another doctor at the hospital on Monday.

Me: No, I don't want that.

Him: [more in control now] I still think this baby needs to come out sooner rather than later and I think it should be today.

Me: [reluctantly] Okay, I'll do it then.

Him: So, you will go to the hospital this morning?

Me: Yes, I'll be there at 8.30. I'll see you then.

His final words to me were, *"There's no need to worry, Karin, it's quite safe."*

I woke Jim and told him about the telephone call. Although I had agreed on the phone to be at the hospital at 8:30 am, every cell of my being was on red alert. I told Jim what the obstetrician had said about William needing to come out sooner rather than later and spoke again of my intense feeling of foreboding.

"I really don't want to do this. It doesn't feel good in here," I said quietly, indicating my solar plexus. Then I added, "Plus, it's Samhain. I read up on it and it's an ancient Celtic festival. They believe that the veil between here and the spirit world is thin today."

Jim's next words were ones that I'll never forget: "Are you really going to make decisions about our baby's health based on a pagan ritual?"

To me, it was as though the axe fell right then and there. Both my husband, William's father, and our trusted obstetrician agreed that my baby was being induced to avert possible complications, to ensure his wellbeing. I understood this, but the feeling of doom and foreboding did not diminish. I had many friends whose babies had been induced and all were healthy. If this intervention was being done to ensure William's safety, then logically there was only one other person who could be harmed by it, and that was me.

I farewelled our beautiful daughters, silently wondering if this would be our last kisses and cuddles, willing them to feel my love for them. Their lives would be forever changed if I did not return, and I tried to tell myself to stop imagining things. In the car, my thoughts turned to William. What would happen to a newborn baby boy without a mother? My own father had been one, with my grandmother dying of septicaemia days after giving birth to him. His life had not been easy. Like my grandpa, I knew that Jim would be lost without me, both emotionally and practically, and would need help.

As Jim drove east down High Street, I said quietly, "If anything happens to me today, I need you to promise me that you will stay with the baby and not try to stay with me."

Jim looked at me and scoffed, "Don't be ridiculous."

"Stop the car," I said, but Jim kept driving. "Stop the car! I'm not going. Take me back home right now."

Jim looked stunned. Suddenly the penny dropped that I was completely serious.

"What do you mean?" he said.

"Promise me now that you will stay with the baby, no matter what happens."

"Okay," he said. "I promise, but nothing is going to happen."

"I really hope not, but I want you to remember what you've promised," I said, feeling calmer now that Jim had given his word. "If anything goes wrong and I can't speak, I need you to remember to stay with William, not me. Don't leave him."

Jim and I arrived at the hospital at 8:30 am, checked in and were escorted to a delivery suite. The midwife, who looked to be nearing retirement age, introduced herself. Despite feeling an initial aversion to her, I rationalised that I should feel reassured by her years of experience. I changed and she did a CTG to measure William's heart rate. A CTG (cardiotocograph) consists of a belt strapped around the mother's abdomen and has two discs on it, one to measure baby's heartrate and the other to measure contractions.

Electrical cords run from the discs to a machine which gives a digital display of the heartrate and can also produce sound. Most importantly, the machine also produces a printout which shows the baby's heartrate and how it changes with contractions. William's heartrate was looking good. Completely normal. The CTG was removed and we then sat around waiting for the obstetrician to arrive.

When he did, he proceeded to artificially rupture the membranes with alligator forceps and had great difficulty doing so, commenting that the membranes were unusually tough. He was digging around and it was causing me discomfort. When he eventually pulled out the instrument, he held it up to the midwife and said, "Is that hair?"

She said, "Yes." I could clearly see a tuft of dark hair sticking out of the end of the instrument. He had pulled William's hair out by the roots. William's first experience of the outside world was the pain of having his hair ripped out of his head and at the same time losing the safety and comfort of the amniotic fluid that had cushioned him throughout his life to that point.

The obstetrician said that he would return late morning to see how things were progressing, then left. The amount of amniotic fluid that came out was far more than either of my previous pregnancies and even the midwife commented on the amount.

There was no sign of labour as a result of the artificial rupture of the membranes. All that morning, William moved about inside me and was obviously still healthy. I was on the phone to Sherrin, ensuring that Valerie would get to the airport as arranged and also to Lisa, who would look after the girls when Valerie left. Jim did the cryptic crossword in the newspaper and gave me the quiz, just as we did every day.

By late morning, it was obvious that further measures would need to be taken. Lunchtime came and went, and we wondered when the obstetrician would arrive. Sometime later, the midwife called out from another room and said that the obstetrician wanted to know what we would like to do now. I had no idea why they were asking me this. I'd never wanted to be induced. This was their show, not mine. The only two ways of chemical induction that I knew of, that the obstetrician had mentioned at an earlier appointment, were a gel to soften the cervix or a drip to bring on contractions. I felt that things had dragged on long enough and was concerned about William being left sitting without any amniotic fluid so I said that they should proceed with the drip.

Having had two quick labours with no drugs, I deduced that this would be very quick. I gave no thought to pain relief other than that if I really needed it, I would ask for an epidural. I had no knowledge of any increased risks with induction. Nor had my pregnancy books said anything about the risks involved other than to say that, if medical intervention became necessary, I should put myself into the hands of the medical staff and trust their judgement. That is what I did.

The obstetrician arrived to administer the drip. According to the records, it was 2:00 pm. He then left immediately. The midwife recorded that she commenced the synthetic oxytocin at 2:20 pm. I had told the midwife that I hated being hooked up to the CTG as I like to walk through contractions. She told me to call her when contractions commenced. She also said to let her know if I needed pain relief, then left the room.

I made a final phone call to my Aunt Valerie at our home from the hospital phone in the labour suite telling her that the drip had gone in and organising final details of when Lisa would take over the babysitting from her later that afternoon. In 2003, landlines were still in use and I had no idea at the time how vitally important the timing of that phone call was, nor how important being able to prove it would become months and years down the track.

## Chapter Seven

# Angel Came Today

*"When you doubt your power, you give power to your doubt."*
*~ Honore de Balzac*

I felt the first contractions soon after the drip went in but did not immediately tell the midwife as I knew that she would strap me to the CTG. It quickly became apparent to me that induced labour was going to be very different from my previous birth experiences as the pain was already stronger than any I had known before, and the contractions were so unrelenting as to be almost constant. I also resolved to ask the midwife about an epidural for pain relief, such was the intensity of labour pain, but I never got the opportunity to do so.

Had anyone given us even a basic explanation of the need for continuous monitoring during artificially induced labour, I would have had that thing strapped to me from the time my waters were artificially broken. As it was, I tried to hold out for 3:00 pm but couldn't. I called out to the midwife and she came in trundling the

CTG machine along and proceeded to hook me up. She said that I could disconnect myself to go to the toilet.

We recall that it was not long before Jim noticed that the digital readout would go along at about 140 then dip to 90. After the third time this happened, Jim called out to the midwife because she was not in the room with us and asked her if that should be happening. Later, under oath, the midwife said she does not recall what alerted her to an abnormal CTG.

She came in to look and appeared concerned. She told me to get on the bed, then put an oxygen mask on me. At some stage she turned off the drip. She observed the CTG, then tore off the paper trace and went, we assumed, to call the obstetrician. The midwife continued to come and go from the room. She would ask me to change position and check the CTG trace.

We sat there looking at each other and Jim pulled out the video camera. I could see him fiddling with it, in preparation for filming. In retrospect, this would have been the best thing that could have happened because the video would have provided a date and time stamp – something that should have been on the CTG trace but wasn't. It looked like it went on briefly but wasn't filming so Jim plugged it in to charge. We'd been so busy lately that neither of us had thought to charge the battery.

Jim and I watched as William's heart rate deteriorated before our eyes and wondered how much longer the obstetrician would take to get there. We had assumed that the midwife had contacted him when she first became concerned but never actually asked if she had done so. William's heartbeat began to dip so alarmingly that Jim yelled out, "Where the hell is the doctor?" The midwife, who was not in the room, called out that he was on the way. Even then, it felt like it was still a long time before he arrived.

At some stage, I asked the midwife to do an internal examination as I believed that the intensity of the contractions would indicate imminent birth. I was crushed when she told me that I was only 2–3 cm dilated.

The obstetrician arrived and said, "What's going on here?"

I replied that I didn't know, but I was all trussed up like a turkey and that I didn't like it. He applied a scalp electrode to William's head through the opening of my cervix. I remember that he went to the side of the bed, slightly behind me and out of my line of sight in the vicinity of the drip machine.

There were a few indeterminate words between the midwife and the obstetrician, then the obstetrician told me that I would be having a caesarean. He said that William wasn't happy in there and needed to come out. He told Jim to go outside for a walk.

The obstetrician left the room, presumably to make phone calls for staff. Meanwhile, the midwife prepared me for theatre and a catheter was inserted. At one stage, she turned me onto my side and William's heart rate stopped. She instantly turned me back. Jim went for his walk outside for fresh air while I was being prepped. The CTG was still going and I watched the digital display of William's heart rate. From my memory, the midwife came and went a few times. There was the time she turned me onto my right side and the heart rate dropped off the screen. There was a time where I distinctly remember being alone and the readout was around 40. The midwife came in, saw I was watching it, took the belt off me and turned it off. She said, "You won't be needing this anymore." Even then, I did not go to theatre and there was a period of time where I just lay there not knowing what was going on, not able to see William's heart rate, and I was so frightened for him. Things seemed to be moving slowly.

I know now that there were no theatre staff, no anaesthetist and no paediatrician on hand. I know now that private hospitals with no Emergency Department usually only have these staff on call. In the event of an emergency, the on-call staff have to be contacted and then travel to the private hospital from their homes or wherever they were at the time. I learned later from the paediatrician that he had been sitting down to dinner.

I cannot overstate the horror of what William went through. Even after they disconnected the CTG and wheeled me on a trolley into theatre, I still did not realise that William might die. I was worried for his health after birth but not his life. I just did not think that babies died during childbirth in this day and age. As they were wheeling me along I kept asking, "Where's Jim? I want him with me!"

The obstetrician said he would get Jim gowned up for theatre. After that, things seemed to move along faster and when I was wheeled into theatre, the anaesthetist said that he was going to turn me on my side. I said to him, "The baby doesn't like it when I'm on my side." The obstetrician was absent from the room but the midwife was present and there was some discussion about equipment not reaching if I wasn't turned on my side. The anaesthetist proceeded with the epidural as William had to come out and those were his instructions from the obstetrician.

Once the epidural was administered, a blue plastic screen was put up over my chest so I could not see my tummy. Jim was sitting at the top of my head, holding my hand. I could feel all the pushing and pulling as they cut me open and pulled William out and I remember feeling like William Wallace being tortured in Braveheart – minus the physical pain. I was crushing Jim's hand and crying silently.

While the caesarean was underway, the phone rang and the anaesthetist answered, saying to the obstetrician , "It's [another obstetrician], he wants to know if you need help." The obstetrician said yes and shortly thereafter, another obstetrician, his relieving colleague who had presumably arrived to do his afternoon rounds, stood across from our obstetrician and assisted him. Time of birth was recorded as 5:53 pm.

I saw the obstetrician cross to where the paediatrician waited and knew that William was born. I waited to hear a gurgle or a cry, waited for someone to tell me that my son was okay but all was silent. The paediatrician proceeded to resuscitate William. I could not see him, but Jim said later he was as white as the sheet on the bed. It was not long after William was handed over that the anaesthetist said something like, "I'm going over to help." Again, there was a sense of urgency to his words. The obstetrician was back to working on my tummy and I could not see anything of William or what was happening to him. That's when I knew that something was very wrong and felt fear as I have never known before. No-one spoke and I whispered to Jim, "Can you see him?" Jim just shook his head, put his head on our clasped hands and I felt his tears on my hand. I said, "Remember what we spoke of, stay with the baby, it's not his fault." He just shook his head and cried.

Our obstetrician did not speak for some time, and I was too frightened to say anything in case I distracted anyone from their task. He eventually spoke over the screen and said, "Karin and Jim, the baby's been born with no heartbeat or pulse. They are working on him now, but it's not looking good, I'm afraid."

I lay there crying quietly and whispered to Jim to go to William. He just shook his head. I said, "Go to him. It's not his fault." Jim just bowed his head and cried. I wanted to get up and go to my baby but I could feel them pushing and pulling me so I knew I couldn't. The first I knew that the operation was over was when the theatre staff were counting instruments and cleaning up. When they finally took the screen away, the two obstetricians had disappeared without saying another word to us. I couldn't understand how our obstetrician could just leave us like that.

I could not move or even lift my head, only roll it to the side trying desperately to catch a glimpse of William across the room. White-gowned and masked people were standing leaning over him blocking my view. I could only see a glimpse of a tiny patch of baby skin between them.

This reality was more hideous than any scene from a horror movie. There we were, three people who love each other more than anything, alone like little islands of agony in a nightmare. All I wanted was to touch my son, to bring him back to us with my love for him, to let him know that I had not abandoned him. Instead, I lay bleeding and paralysed, at the mercy of the people who I felt had utterly failed William.

I wept quietly and begged God to let my baby live. I spoke silently to William's spirit, hoping that he would hear me, sending him my love and asking him to forgive me for letting this happen to him. I promised him that I would always look after him if he would just come back to us but also told him that if he really needed to go that I would understand and always love him. After nearly thirteen minutes, the paediatrician was about to give up when William fought his way back to us.

I cannot remember anything else until they wheeled William over on the trolley to be parallel beside me. The trolley was higher than the table I was on and I could only see his little hand and arm, and a little of his side. I asked for someone to lift my head so I could see him and kiss his hand. I wanted to lift him up and put him straight to my breast. It was all that I knew to do and it had always fixed everything for the girls when they were babies. William was naked on that trolley made for grown-ups and I worried about him being cold. To this day, I wish I could have held him to me and maybe he would have been alright, maybe it was all he needed. If I could have, I would have but I could not even move.

He was totally inert apart from his chest rising and falling. The anaesthetist held a pump attached to a tube which was in William's mouth and he was squeezing the pump in his hand to breathe for William. The paediatrician said something about William now having a heartbeat. His colour was not white but neither was it a healthy pink. I thought that they would take him away and make him better – put him in one of those warm humidicribs that sick babies go into. I had faced the fact that he might be a special needs child but still held hope that he would be unscathed. He was big and looked perfect. I knew he was strong. Either way, I was not prepared for the paediatrician's question.

"Do you want us to continue to resuscitate?"

My mind went blank. What did he mean? Was he saying William might live forever trapped in a lifeless body? Why else would he ask that question? These questions formed out of that blankness, but I could not speak. I looked up and the midwife was at my head, her mask on, looking down at me, upside down, with tears in her eyes.

I said, "What do you think?"

She replied, "I think you have to give him a chance."

I said immediately, "Yes, continue to resuscitate."

The paediatrician told us they would take him to the nursery to continue resuscitation and he said, "He's a fighter, your William."

Then they wheeled him away.

I was taken to a room for recovery where I reminded Jim of his promise made to me in the car to stay with William, no matter what. I asked him to find William and not to leave him. A few minutes later, Jim came back. He said that he couldn't get into the nursery, that the obstetrician had stopped him at the door and told him he couldn't go in. He said all the blinds were pulled down so he couldn't see anything.

I wanted to scream at him to knock down anyone who got in his way, just get back to William but, drugged and traumatised, I could barely manage a whisper. I could see he was a broken man, a traumatised father who could go no further, so we just sat quietly together in shock. Jim did not have it in him to do more, and I was quite literally paralysed, physically and mentally. I had *promised* William that I would always look after him if he came back and now he was alone, his little body being subjected to what I felt was like torturous treatment without anyone who loved him nearby. I felt that I had failed him again and no matter how I rationalise it, that feeling of having failed to protect my baby will be with me forever.

The anaesthetic had caused the sensation of ants crawling under the skin of my upper torso and I lay there paralysed, drugged with morphine, scratching incessantly at my upper body, weeping silently, my mind reaching for William. The nurses constantly monitored me and applied something that soothed the itching. My physical body was there, but it was just a shell. My mind and heart were constantly reaching out to William. This was when I could sense William's terror. Still psychically connected as mother and baby, I could feel his pain and fear, like screaming inside me. It went on and on, then it would stop. Then it would start again. It was hours before we had word. I saw hell that day and fought silently in those long, agonising hours to prevent William from being taken by it.

I have no idea of what time it was or how long we were there. I have snatches of memories of the paediatrician talking to me but can't say if it was once or twice. I remember him referring to William as "stillborn" but can't remember if that was in the theatre or later in recovery. During this time, other nurses were caring for me. One of them was an agency nurse (meaning she was like a temp called in to cover for permanent staff). She asked me what had happened to my baby, and I told her that he was stillborn but was being resuscitated in the nursery. She told me, quite adamantly, that he was not stillborn if he breathed. The obstetrician did not come near us. Jim was hungry, but it was beyond both of us to think of organising food – or anything at all.

We waited and waited in that hospital room and were told that the NETS (Newborn Emergency Transport Service) team would be called in to stabilise William in readiness for transport to the Mercy Neonatal Intensive Care Unit, referred to as NICU by the medical personnel. The midwife and the NETS team were talking about the paediatrician at Mercy NICU with respect that bordered on awe. Much later, when questions began to surface, I asked why it took so long to call the NETS team. I was told that, due to the cost of mobilising the team – which included a paediatrician, nurse and ambulance officer – the NETS team would only be called if a baby lived for one hour after birth.

The enormity of this was devastating. My interpretation was that any woman giving birth in a hospital that does not have a NICU must accept that her baby will not receive specialist emergency neonatal intensive care, if required, unless the baby lives for an hour after birth. With this knowledge, why would any woman choose a hospital without a NICU? On this basis, William would have been better off if I had given birth at home with an independent midwife. There would have been no induction and, had complications occurred, an ambulance call would have resulted in admission to an emergency department of a public hospital with maternity and neonatal units.

I remember the NETS doctor coming in to tell me that they had stabilised William enough to transport him to the Mercy. She also said that William had suffered brain damage and it was probably severe. She explained that William had already had five shots of adrenaline to the heart each time his heart had stopped and that he was now on a continuous, low dose of adrenaline intravenously and it seemed to be holding him. She said that he was on a ventilator and that he was intermittently gasping around the tube but not really breathing for himself and asked us whether we wanted her to continue to give William shots of adrenaline if his heart stopped again. I did not know they had been doing that to him. In that instant, I connected the feelings of terror and the intermittent feelings of loss. We told her not to do that to him anymore but to leave the continuous dose on. It was like torturing a small, defenceless animal in a laboratory. Everything in me screamed for him to stay with us, but I could not condemn William to a life of pain and suffering even though I selfishly wanted him any way I could have him.

The NETS doctor said that they would bring William in so I could see him and touch him through an opening in the side of the incubator he would be in. She described it to me so I would be prepared and told me that there would be a lot of wires connected to William. They asked if we would like him baptised and we said yes.

I also remember the man in the NETS team popping his head in and saying, "Your son has just done an enormous poo!" I felt sick because I thought that he must have been so frightened.

They brought William in and I got to touch him. A different midwife baptised him with water in a little, stainless steel jug. He lay inert with wires everywhere and the tube coming out of his mouth. There were bright lights above him and I remember thinking that at least they would keep him warm now. I still just wanted to take all that hideous stuff off him and cuddle him to me. I was sure that if I did, William would open his eyes and look up at me.

Instead, they wheeled him away and Jim left to follow the ambulance in our car. The NETS team left me a brochure which I did not read for over two years. It explains what NETS is and it had the names of the team written in biro inside.

I wanted to go with William, but that was not possible. I was still in recovery from the caesarean, unable to walk and attached to a drip, so there was no room for me in the NETS vehicle. I lay there, my mind and heart connected to William, begging and willing him to stay with us, to not give up, to live.

Then a call came from the doctor at the Mercy to get William's mother over there, *now*, and an ambulance was called. When they arrived, there was some discussion between the nurse and the paramedics about the pump attached to my drip. The pump belonged to the private hospital, and they would not hand it over to the ambulance. The ambulance didn't have a pump. I listened as though in a nightmare, still speaking silently to William and begging him to stay with me.

The midwives bundled up my belongings, put my coat over me on the trolley and I was loaded into an ambulance to the Mercy. The video camera was sitting on top of my hospital bag. Someone must have unplugged the charger in the delivery suite and put the camera on top of the bag. It was late at night and the air was cold. The ambulance officers were nice, but I was not really present, trying as I was to connect with William's spirit. There was no more terror. It was difficult to feel him. He had gone to that other place where he'd gone periodically during resuscitation. I decided never to will him back to me again, knowing now that I would be calling him back to suffer. My recollections of that sombre drive are of surreal, distorted flashes of streetlights and car headlights through the windows, reflected on the ceiling. The smell of stale cigarette smoke on the ambulance officer riding quietly beside me in the back. There was nothing to say, no small talk to be had. It was all too sad.

Eventually, I was unloaded and wheeled into the Mercy hospital in East Melbourne. My arrival at the NICU was even more surreal. Still on the ambulance trolley, I was greeted by a man whose wild, red hair and beard made him look like he had just come down from the Scottish Highlands. He introduced himself and then said the words, "I'm someone you never want to meet."

The penny dropped. This must be the doctor they had been screaming genius on at the private hospital. This was the man who now held William's life in his hands. They wheeled me over to the crib to see William. My son was beautiful, heartbreakingly so. He looked like a male version of Holly and Bonnie as newborns, except that William was born with a head of curly dark hair and finely shaped dark eyebrows. Long, dark eyelashes fanned his cheeks. William never opened his eyes, but I know he was the tall, dark-haired, blue-eyed son that I'd dreamed of. He was utterly still, apart from the rise and fall of his chest as the machine breathed for him.

Jim was sitting beside William eating sandwiches from a plastic packet. A part of my brain registered that he had finally gotten to eat. The room was dim and quiet. There were other cribs in the room which I assumed held sick babies, but there was no sound coming from them.

The doctor was talking to me. He recapped what had occurred at the other hospital, told me that William was severely brain damaged and that he did not expect William to live through the night. His words were, strangely, no surprise to me. I knew William was already gone. I could feel his spirit far away, still connected to me but gone from here.

The ambulance personnel had been kind and patient, but they needed their trolley back. I was transferred to a wheelchair, so exhausted that I could barely hold my head up. The doctor had arranged a bed for me on the ward upstairs and I was to be taken there to get some rest while William would be taken for a brain scan. If William's condition changed, he told me I would be brought downstairs immediately.

The wheelchair had just pulled up beside the bed on the ward when a nurse appeared and spoke in urgent, hushed tones. I was to return to NICU immediately. The wheelchair was turned around and I was rushed downstairs. William's heart had stopped for the final time, the breathing tube was removed, and my baby boy was given back to me at around 12:30 am on 2 November 2003. He was limp, not moving at all. There was a lot of clear mucus coming from his nose. I wanted to breast feed him, to pull down the private hospital gown and squirt the colostrum already filling my breasts into his mouth. Immediately after that thought, came another, "Oh wait. His nose is blocked with mucus and he'll suffocate if I feed him." Even as I thought it, I could see William was not breathing at all. A scream of horror and denial welled up inside me, threatening to consume me and I clamped it down fiercely, mindful of those other cots in the unit.

I got to hold him for the first time as he died in my arms with Jim's arms around us both, my tears bathing William's head, telling him over and over how very much I love him. With every inhalation, I drew in the scent of William's head, trying to commit it to memory so I would never forget the unique smell of my baby son. I didn't know it at the time, but the doctor was taking photos. He knew what we did not – that those photos would become the most precious of treasures. There would be no cute baby portraits for our William, no first bath photos, no smiles, no crawling, no first steps or first day of school. Nothing. All we have are the handful of photos taken by this wonderful man. Photos of William as he died, cradled in the arms of his weeping mummy and daddy.

William tried so hard to stay with us and it was truly horrible what the doctors and nurses had to do to try to save him. He never breathed continuously for himself or opened his eyes – I don't even know for sure what colour they were. My life changed irrevocably from that moment and neither Jim nor I would ever be the same people again.

I spent that night with William in my hospital room. Although it was the early hours of Sunday morning when William's baby body was handed to me in bed, it still feels like the longest night of my life. Jim had left to go home to be with the girls and would bring them in to see their little brother in the morning. I lay on the narrow hospital bed with my baby in my arms, knowing that this would be my only night to hold and cuddle him. I was more tired than I could ever remember being before, my body having endured intense, artificially induced labour followed by an emergency caesarean, which is major abdominal surgery, and unimaginable trauma. The physical would heal eventually but the trauma would stay with me forever.

I kept nodding off over William as I cradled him in my arms and worried that I might fall asleep and drop him. I'd been told that I could not lift my baby after the caesarean section and that I would need to call a nurse to move William. A nurse came to help me and put William in the clear Perspex crib, pushing it close to my bed so I could reach out and touch him. That is how I dozed for short periods, with my arm stretched out over the hard edge of the plastic crib, until the doctor came in during the wee hours. Apologising for the intrusion, he went on to say that he had been on the phone fighting with the coroner's office for the past 2–3 hours. Someone had reported William's death to the coroner and the coroner wanted to take William's body to be autopsied. Now.

The scream in my solar plexus threatened to erupt and I clamped down on it even harder. William's poor little baby body was already battered, punctured and bruised from what had occurred during resuscitation. Thoughts of his skull being sawn open, his chest being cut and his organs pulled out for examination made me want to crouch over his body like a wild animal and fight to the death anyone who came to take him from me.

I told the doctor that I would not consent, but he replied that the coroner does not require consent to conduct an autopsy. He said he had already spoken with the coroner's office at length, advocating on my behalf even before I knew anything about it. He knew that I needed time with my baby, that our family needed to spend some time with William. They had agreed to allow me to keep William with me for the night, but they would be coming to take his body in the morning. I asked if there was any way to stop this happening and he said that I could write an objection to the coroner, requesting no autopsy be performed. I wrote and signed it right then and there, in the darkest hours of the night.

I knew nothing about the coroner's office or the coronial system. I did not understand that, if someone had reported William's death in the middle of the night, it was because they believed the circumstances of his death warranted investigation. I do not know who spoke up for my baby son that night, but they have my enduring gratitude for their integrity and courage in coming forward.

Alone in the night with my dead baby's bruised body, there was nobody to advise me of what might lay ahead. Nobody to tell me that the time would come when I would have questions and that I would have to navigate what turned out for me to be a ruthless, highly organised medico-legal system. There was nobody there to tell me that an autopsy would be necessary to prove that my baby had died from his brain being starved of oxygen. Nobody there to advise me that the absence of autopsy could cast doubts on the cause of death that was written on William's death certificate.

Most people in the same position would feel the same but I have lived to regret it and advise anyone in a similar situation to always allow an autopsy. I still have a copy of the form. At the time, I felt like I was protecting William. When I look at it now, it feels like I failed:

**FORM A. REQUEST BY A SENIOR NEXT OF KIN TO A CORONER NOT TO DIRECT AN AUTOPSY**

Re: William Grant Keays, Deceased

I do not believe that performing an autopsy on my baby's body is necessary. It is obvious that he died of hypoxia & feel that any further information would be obtained from examining the placenta. I object to my baby's body being interfered with in any way and do not want any part of him removed. It would greatly distress me.

Signed: K. Keays
Date: 2-11-03

As the grey morning light dawned, I asked the nurse to bring William's body out of the crib so I could unwrap him. What I saw made me want to weep and wail in horror and despair. Black, blue and red contusions covered his poor little body. What had been done to him? What had he endured in his tiny, short life?

I asked the nurse, "What are these marks?"

She looked sadly at me and said, "I don't know."

*Do you want us to continue to resuscitate?* Those words came back to me now. I had no idea what that meant to William at the time, I still did not know. Right now, all I could see was the outcome, the aftermath, the results of the physical actions upon my innocent baby's body.

The weight of my answer settled upon me, breaking my heart and burning my brain.

*Continue to resuscitate.* Those were my words, uttered whilst trying to keep my baby alive. Those same words unwittingly condemned my baby to a short life of pain and terror. Tears of sorrow and grief fell from my eyes onto my beautiful little boy as I gently touched and kissed his bruises, whispering, "I'm so sorry, I'm so sorry, I'm so sorry… please forgive me… I'm so sorry."

Jim brought the girls in early that morning to see their baby brother. At eight years old, Holly cradled her baby brother in her arms just as she had cradled Bonnie as a baby, and would not let him go. Her stricken, white, little face tore at my heart. How could I comfort my daughter? I had no reference for this. There was no way for me to make this okay for her.

At just two years old, Bonnie was still a toddler. Lying in the hospital bed, I watched her walk up to gaze silently at William.

Her child's face held the wisdom and compassion of an archangel. She lifted her little hand and ever so gently touched William's bruised mouth with a slender finger and said, "Baby, ouch."

Even as my heart clenched with grief and sadness, she toddled around the foot of my bed and came to stand at the bedside. Rising onto tiptoes, Bonnie reached her hand up to mine, which rested on the bed. Raising her beautiful, green eyes to mine she softly touched the back of my hand where the drip went in and said, "Mummy, ouch."

We have a family photo of us all together in that room. Holly is holding William and I am in bed trying to muster a smile for the family portrait. Years later, Holly would question me on why I was smiling. I have no answer for that other than that I remember thinking this was to be our only family photo with the five of us together and my traumatised brain, as yet unable to fully accept that William was dead, was trying to make it a nice one.

Jim and the girls went home as we did not want them to see William being taken away. Two men in black arrived. They gently and respectfully laid William in a baby's carry cot, then zipped it up and took him away.

## Chapter Eight

## Will Ye No' Come Back Again?

*"Youth fades, love droops, the leaves of friendship fall; A mother's secret hope outlives them all."*
~ Oliver Wendell Holmes

The moment that William's body disappeared through the doorway with the undertakers, I wanted to return to the private hospital. William was gone. I did not feel him here at all in this hospital, even though it was where he had passed on. The doctor and nurses at the Mercy NICU were amazing professionals whose care for William and me was faultless. Their holistic care extended to our whole family and they were incredibly compassionate and supportive. They encouraged me to stay with them for as long as I needed to recover. I could see that they did not understand why I wanted to return there but, to me, it was where William had died many times over. I wanted to be there to understand what had happened.

Instinctively, I already knew that I needed to forgive everyone and everything associated with William's death or it would destroy me. Something had gone terribly wrong and I wanted to understand what had happened so I could forgive. Jim had already begun to express his anger at the obstetrician and private hospital and I shut him down, telling him that everyone had done their best. Even my beloved Aunt Valerie, calling from Queensland, was angry at the obstetrician, telling me outright that "they killed him." I told her firmly that everyone had done their best and that I didn't want to hear any recriminations. It was the only time in my life that I ever challenged her on anything. Valerie said sadly that she supposed she would have to find a way to stop being angry and do what I had asked of her. Later, with time to process everything that had unfolded, it became clear to me that Jim and Valerie were right to ask questions. It no longer seemed to me that everyone had done their best. At this time though, less than 24 hours since I'd held William as he died, I was a deeply traumatised woman in every way – physically, emotionally, mentally and spiritually.

The Mercy staff had dressed William in donated clothes and bunny rugs. In the crib, he had been tucked up beneath a beautiful hand-stitched patchwork quilt. On the underside of the quilt, a pink heart is stitched onto the lining. Handwritten on the heart is the inscription, 'A Cherished Memory Quilt ~96~'. The quilt travelled with me, back to the private hospital, in a small box. The box was painted inside and out in turquoise and distressed with gold paint on all sides. On the lid were two white doves and on the base a sticker that read 'Purple Palette', which I assumed was the business name of its maker. Along with the quilt, there was a handmade booklet. The first page reads:

Baby's Name: William Keays
Weight: 9lb 7oz, 4272 g
Length: 58.5 cm
Head circumference: 36 cm
Colour of hair: Brown

The next pages had William's hand and footprints, a lock of his hair, a wrist tag and polaroid photos of William before and after his passing. The box also held William's yellow plastic government-issued ChildHealth record booklet, just like Holly's and Bonnie's except there was only one page completed with his birth details.

The box and its contents were instantly precious beyond measure to me. I was told later that the quilt and box were handmade by women who had lost children of their own. I thought of the hours of love and care that would have gone into selflessly creating these items for unknown women such as myself, knowing that one day they would be needed and treasured. I do not know who these women are, but wish I could thank them and let them know how grateful I am for their kindness, and how sorry I am for their loss.

As soon as I arrived back at the private hospital, I asked to see the obstetrician and the midwife and was told that the midwife was taking time off. Sherrin arrived with an enormous soft toy bought for William in anticipation of his birth, just as she had done for the birth of each of our children. My dear friend sat at my bedside on the left and we cried together quietly. She told me a long time afterwards, months maybe years, that she looked at me and thought, How are you still breathing? I don't know how you are able to sit up in that bed.

There was nothing else to do or say. The obstetrician walked in while she was there and sat down on the other side of the bed, directly across from Sherrin. He sat in the chair with an edginess about him, as though expecting to be attacked, then proceeded to speak in a quavering voice, as though he'd memorised a script. He said that he had gone over everything that had occurred yesterday and there was nothing that could have been done differently. He then told me he had no doubt at all that William would be dead inside me now if he had not induced me yesterday. While he was mouthing the words, I watched him with blank, numb detachment and didn't believe him. I told him that the coroner had taken William and he slumped. When I told him I had written to the coroner, objecting to William being autopsied, he seemed to spring up in his seat, looking much relieved. Then he checked himself and added that he would ask the coroner that my wishes be honoured. His whole demeanour changed immediately as I watched him with that same detachment.

Snezana was in Melbourne visiting her family and was booked to fly back to the States on 2 November. She had planned to visit me in hospital and meet Billy before leaving but now she was torn between wanting to stay to support me and needing to leave to honour her commitments in the States. Never, in all our years of friendship, had we envisioned that we would be doing anything like this. I told her there was nothing she could do to help me and that she should go. There was nothing anyone could do. William was dead and that was all I knew. Inside, I was still with William, replaying every second, every single moment of the previous days, searching for a way out of the hell in which we now found ourselves. It was as though there was a door tantalisingly close to my fingertips, if only I could identify it. The door that would turn back time and make everything right, the door that would bring my baby back to me.

An enormous flower arrangement arrived from Snezana and Logan. It was the only one on those first days after William's birth.

My stay at the private hospital after William's birth and death was very different from the last time with Bonnie, when my room had been bursting with flowers, balloons, visitors and gifts. This time, I was not in the maternity ward but in a single room far down the end of a corridor. I had spent my pregnancy looking forward to that magical time in hospital bonding with my newborn son just as I had with Holly and Bonnie. But that would never happen. Instead of breastfeeding William and sleeping with him beside me, I had only empty arms and memories that were the stuff of horror movies. That Sunday night on the day William died, alone in the dark, I existed in an agonised miasma of horror, misery and unutterable grief. My baby was gone, but where? His body was in the coroner's morgue, but where was his soul? I wanted only to be with William to care for him, to make sure he was alright. It was not that I wanted to die; it was just that I needed to be with my baby. I couldn't really sleep. I didn't want to breathe, but my body kept breathing of its own accord. I waited for my broken, lacerated, agonised heart to simply stop beating, but it would not.

A midwife appeared and sat with me. She spoke of the loss of her own baby girl many years ago. Holding my hand, she stayed with me most of that night, sometimes just sitting quietly beside me or bringing me a hot drink. I will never forget her kindness – she was like an angel sent to guide me through the darkest of nights.

My body was very different after this unnatural birth by medical intervention. Planned caesarean section is major abdominal surgery, with a slower recovery time than natural birth. Like any surgery or medical procedure, it comes with its own set of risks and side effects, which is one of the reasons why I had assiduously avoided medical intervention with my girls. Emergency caesareans, though, are unplanned, which means that the urgency of getting the baby out of the womb is paramount. A C-section involves two incisions, one through the abdominal wall and another through the uterus itself. The baby is removed through the incisions, which are then stitched up. That is two different wounds of around 10 cm in length, with two lots of stitches, one you can see and the other you can't because it's internal. When a woman holds her living, breathing newborn baby for the first time, physical trauma falls away and is erased from her mind by love and gratitude for the blessing of the new life in her arms. Not for me, not this time.

In being induced, I'd allowed the obstetrician to perform an intervention that had instinctively been anathema to me. My body felt violated and battered from the induction and emergency caesarean, but that was of little consequence to me. Still in a state of shock, I felt it was all I deserved. William had paid the ultimate price for whatever had gone on. His traumatised and bruised little body, the terror and fear that I had felt from him, these were the things that haunted me. I was still alive and William was not. I'd had the premonition, rationalised it but got it wrong. If anyone had to die, it should have been me.

In that room down the corridor, I felt like a pariah, a freak put far away from other mums and babies. Days later, when I ventured slowly and painfully from the room to go for a walk, I noted the look of alarm on the face of a nurse as I passed by the nursery. What did they think? That I was going to grab a baby or something? I didn't want anybody else's baby. I wanted my William, whose poor little body was now somewhere across town with the coroner. The sound of a newborn crying was like a knife in my already lacerated heart and I made sure that I never walked that way again.

Jim brought the girls to visit daily, but it wasn't much fun for them so they didn't stay long. Jim would also come alone during the day to sit with me and take me for walks, which was part of the recovery process from surgery. I would lean on his arm and we would walk quietly around the corridors. One sunny day, he took me outside into the garden and we found a seat near the hospital entrance. Sitting together quietly, holding hands, we saw the midwife from William's birth, dressed in uniform, walking up the driveway. She paused and looked as though she didn't know what to do, before greeting us. It was a brief conversation, stilted, and she obviously could not wait to move on.

Russell Morris came to visit the next day. Sitting at my bedside with tears streaming down his face, there wasn't much to be said. He simply sat with me in the face of my grief, showing his support by being present and letting me see his own sadness.

Liz, our friend from Cardiology nights in Thornbury, came to visit. She had brought their daughter, Elle, with her to look after the girls. They'd walked up to the local shops and Liz had bought Beanie Kids for the girls. She'd also bought one for me, a little bear dressed as a medieval knight. His name was Lancelot and there was a crest on his tabard with the initials BK. He had little gauntlets on this hands and boots on his feet. Liz told me the story of how she'd chosen Lancelot, or how Lancelot had chosen me. She'd been looking at a Highland dancing bear when Lancelot caught her eye. Liz said her hand felt guided to him and she thought, Karin needs a champion.

As she spoke, I listlessly opened the cardboard tag attached to his ear, thinking that BK were also Bonnie's initials. Beanie Kids and Beanie Babies are collectibles. Each has its own name, birthdate and star sign on the tag. However, the toys lose their value to collectors if their tag is removed or damaged. My aching heart jolted when I read Lancelot's tag.

"Liz!" I interrupted her. "Have you looked at this tag?"

"No?" Liz looked a bit nonplussed.

"Lancelot the Bear. Birthday: 1st November. Scorpio!" I read out loud to her, "Did you know this one has William's birthday?"

Liz had not known, but she wasn't surprised either. She had been drawn to Lancelot from the moment she saw him. Later that night, once again unable to sleep, a nurse came to sit with me. I was telling her the story of Lancelot and she remarked that he was a very special bear, indeed, especially with the initials BK on his chest. I looked at her and she said, "Would you ever have called William Billy?"

I couldn't believe that I had not made the connection! Jim, Holly, Bonnie and I had referred to William as Billy ever since we chose the name. We had actually decided to call him Billy Keays from the start, keeping William as his formal name. Now, here was a medieval knight with my wee Billy Keays' initials emblazoned over his heart with the same birthdate, sent to be my champion. It felt like a message to me from my son. I held him to my aching, broken heart and drifted off to sleep with him in my arms, arms that were no longer quite so desolate and empty.

The most surprising visitor was the paediatrician who had cared for William in the NICU. He called ahead to arrange a time to visit me in the private hospital. I wondered why. When he arrived and sat at my bedside, it soon became apparent that he was there because he genuinely cared about William and about my welfare. I detected no underlying motive, no self-serving reason for his being there. Technically, as a paediatrician, he was William's doctor. Yet this doctor was simply doing what we always hope that our doctors will do: he was caring for his patient holistically. Until William's birth and death, mother and baby were as one. The fact that he took time out of his day to travel across town to another hospital out of care for my mental and emotional wellbeing was humbling.

I didn't have many visitors, which was probably a good thing as I was incapable of making polite small talk, anyway. My friend Carmel arrived one day. The door half opened and her dear face peeked around from behind it.

"I'm so sorry!" The words were out of my mouth before I could think.

Carmel looked alarmed and said, "Not a good time?"

She looked ready to leave and I blurted out, "No! I mean I'm sorry because I just farted. Nothing's been right down there since the caesarean."

She smiled and came into the room. Placing a gift bag of French toiletries on the bedside table, she leaned over to kiss me and said, "What's a fart between friends?"

It was so good to see her.

Another visitor was the lady from the funeral home. I'd never been involved in arranging anyone's funeral before and had no capacity to begin with my own baby son's. Physically, emotionally and psychologically traumatised, the shocking reality of his funeral was so confronting that it was almost too much to bear. Julie said she would liaise with the coroner's office for the release of William's body into their care. It was something that hadn't even occurred to me. This woman's air of competency and compassion gave me a sense of assurance that I could leave this with her and that all the details would be taken care of.

The hospital physiotherapist came to give me a set of exercises suitable for my post-caesarean tummy. I sat with my head on the table that was over my hospital bed. As she talked, I stayed in that position, willing her to cease talking. Her voice droned on and all I could think was that my baby was dead. I didn't care at all if my body resumed shape or not and resented being forced to divert my thoughts from William.

Although the private hospital was doing everything by the book when it came to my post-natal care, I knew that I was not really wanted there. My requests to speak with the midwife were deflected. The obstetrician was on his planned leave so his daily rounds were covered by his colleague, the same one who had arrived during William's birth and called on the phone offering to help. It would be some time before it occurred to me to question the reason for this synchronicity: why the covering doctor had arrived at that particular time. Conversely, the longer I stayed in that room down the end of the corridor, the more I did not want to go home. I just wanted to be with William and so I stayed right where he'd been born.

Jim said he needed me and missed me. He wanted me to come home. He said the girls needed me. I didn't feel capable of functioning as a wife and mother. The outside world was frightening to me. Here, in this sad little cave, I could exist in my own world with my memories. The thought of leaving and returning to our family home without William terrified me.

Eventually, a date was set by Jim and the hospital. On the day before discharge, a noisy machine began to beep incessantly in the next room. I was leaving the next day so didn't mention it to the nurses, thinking that the patient next door must be a very sick person to need such constant monitoring. What had previously been a quiet sanctuary became a form of mental torture that continued throughout the night. By morning, I was almost ready to walk in next door and pull the plug out myself. Jim and the girls came to get me and I looked into the darkened room next door as I walked past. The machine was there, beeping away, but the perfectly made bed was empty.

I still remember the feeling of that sunny spring day as Jim helped me into the car. The girls were so happy to be taking me home. The air smelled fresh and the colours of nature, the green leaves, colourful flowers, green grass and blue sky, seemed slightly unreal as I observed through eyes that felt like those of an alien from another world.

When the car pulled up out front of our home, the scent of the blossoms and roses in our front garden hit me. The sun felt warm on my shoulders as I walked slowly through the front gate, and the sense of disconnection and dread that had held me in thrall fell away. It felt like our beautiful house was opening its arms and enfolding me in its embrace. I was home and wanted nothing more than to sink into my white wicker rocking chair on the verandah, letting the beauty of our garden wash over me and soothe my bewildered, aching soul.

I was sitting quietly on that chair a few days later, rocking gently back and forth listening to the soft buzz of bees as they flew languidly between blossoms. A car pulled up out front, then an enormous bunch of Oriental lillies appeared on the other side of the front gate, in a pink made so vibrant by the sunshine that it was almost psychedelic. A familiar blonde head popped out from the giant bouquet, dark Wayfarers sitting on a tanned, impossibly handsome face that was today missing its customary brilliant white smile.

Darryl Cotton stood on the other side of the gate, paused and looked at me sadly before quietly asking, "How are you doing, kiddo?"

I stopped rocking for a few moments before resuming. His quiet sadness and genuine empathy almost undid me. Darryl was one of the nicest, most genuinely kind-hearted and caring men I've ever known.

"Hey Daz," I said softly, unable to muster up even a semblance of a smile. With Darryl, bravado wasn't needed anyway. "Come on in."

He opened the gate and walked up onto the verandah, dropping a kiss on my head before taking a seat on the matching two-seater lounge to my right. There we sat, sheltered from the afternoon heat by the shade of the verandah and he laid the flowers on the table, removing his sunglasses. His eyes held sadness and helplessness, but mostly they held love and kindness. We sat talking a little, while he just he just sat with me, being present in the face of my grief, while I rocked back and forth. Darryl Cotton was truly an extraordinary man.

*

William had died on a Saturday that was not only Samhain, it was also on the weekend before the Melbourne Cup. Race day is always the first Tuesday in November and the day itself is a public holiday in Melbourne. Many offices are closed on the Monday to give staff a four-day weekend. This meant that, although William's body had been taken on Sunday morning, the objection to autopsy would not be looked at before Wednesday. The coroner ultimately agreed not to perform an autopsy; however, some forensic samples were taken. The delayed process meant that it was an extended period before William's body was released and this was why

William's funeral was set for 13 November, eleven days after his death.

I still wasn't allowed to lift anything heavier than a baby for several weeks due to the caesarean. Bonnie was still used to me lifting her for cuddles, but that had to happen sitting down for six weeks until the wound healed. And like anyone else who has had a caesarean, I wasn't supposed to drive until healed. These were all constant reminders that I had given birth, but I had no baby.

At the time of William's birth, Holly was eight and Bonnie was two. Nothing in the baby and childbirth books prepares you for what to say to your children when their baby brother dies. Nor does life prepare you for how to support them through it. The girls had been very aware of William throughout pregnancy. I would sit down with them every week or so and we would look at the pictures and diagrams in the baby and childbirth book. The book had photos of babies in the womb at each stage of pregnancy so the girls could visualise what our Billy might look like and how his body was growing. I encouraged them to get up close to talk and sing to him in my tummy and when he began moving, they would put their hands on my belly to feel him kick. We were a family of five long before Billy was born and he always will remain part of our family.

To this day, I am forever grateful for the NICU paediatrician's insistence that the coroner's unit did not take William until the morning. He knew, from experience, that our whole family needed to spend as much time with William as possible to begin accepting the reality of his death. When I left home on the morning of 1 November to go to the hospital, we all expected the girls to be meeting their baby brother the next time they saw me. Whilst that was still true in one sense, holding his dead body was not how we had all imagined and anticipated that visit would be for so many months.

Holly and Bonnie understood that William was dead. They did not know how or why he had died and, at that stage, neither did we. The fact that he was dead was enough to process. Jim and I both wanted the girls to feel comfortable speaking freely about William at any time, that they could share their feelings and that they could ask any questions and we would always answer openly and honestly. Early on, I explained to them that I would always be sad about William's death and that I would cry sometimes because I miss him, and that was okay, just like it was okay for them to cry when they felt sad. I was conscious of letting them set the pace, as their sadness and grief was going to be a vastly different experience from my own. But I often did put on a brave face for them. The last thing I wanted to do was remind them of their own sadness in showing my grief.

I still looked pregnant. My body seemed to not know how to restore itself in the same way it had the first two times. Every day, I silently gave thanks to the nurse at the Mercy who had offered me a single dose tablet to dry up my breastmilk before it came in. At least I did not have to cope with the anguish of my body producing milk for my baby.

It took me a few days to work up the courage to venture out to the local shops for bread. I donned my maternity pants, loose top, wide-brimmed floppy hat and sunglasses and prayed that nobody would try to say hello. I dreaded being expected to make small talk. As I trudged up the street, I noticed a school mum walking towards me. She was looking at me with tears in her eyes. I froze, not knowing how to do this, but I had nothing to worry about. Eyes filled with love and kindness, she opened her arms and hugged me, simply saying, "I'm so sorry."

The compassion and grace of this woman chased away my fears and I forced myself to walk daily to the shops, just as I had always done before William. I felt that keeping up the appearance of normality for the girls was important in minimising the impact on their lives.

One day, I was waiting my turn in the bakery when an older woman standing next to me indicated my belly and asked how much longer I had to go? Suddenly, everything seemed to freeze in the bustling shop. You could have heard a pin drop. I looked up and saw the stricken face of the lady behind the counter and answered, "I had my baby last week."

The woman looked slightly embarrassed then asked brightly, "A girl or a boy?"

It was one of those moments in time that seem to stretch out forever. This conversation could go very badly if the well-meaning woman kept asking questions. A part of my mind wondered why I was even considering her feelings, but I was. Another part wanted to turn on her and shriek that my baby was dead. I needed to shut this down fast, so I looked back at her and said, "A little boy."

Then I turned away and quickly stepped up to the counter to order my bread. The lady serving me had tears in her eyes. I kept my head down while she sliced and bagged the bread, then made a swift exit without looking at the older lady again.

It was in that period between coming home from hospital and William's funeral that I answered the phone on my office desk one day. There were daily calls from family and friends as well as the funeral director. Our business contacts were aware of what we were going through and I was a little surprised when a male voice asked to speak with Jim. We had an unlisted phone number, so it was unusual for people to call without greeting me, knowing our office was run from home.

"May I ask who's speaking?" was my standard response to unknown callers.

When he answered, I recognised the name immediately, although we had not met. It was one of the applicants for the Trademark of Masters Apprentices, which we were currently disputing.

As though looking at myself from outside, I marvelled at my apparent composure. My voice remained neutral, businesslike. Inside, I was furious at the intrusion into our home and privacy, especially now. Our son had died only days earlier and had not even had his funeral, his body not yet been laid to rest.

"Is this regarding the Trademark?" I asked.

"Yes," came the reply.

"How did you get this number?" I asked evenly.

"I interviewed Jim on the radio some time ago and had the number from then," he replied. He went on to say he was hoping to speak with Jim to come to an arrangement about the Trademark.

I wanted to scream at him that my baby was dead! I wanted to shriek and curse and tell him how my baby's body had looked when I was forced to hand him to the undertakers, all battered and bruised and DEAD! I wanted to yell and wail at him for being so self-serving, greedy and moneygrubbing as to even think that he had any right at all to the name of Masters Apprentices. I wanted to demand to know why he thought it was okay to try to claim that he has rights to the Trademark (a dispute that was costing us thousands, thanks to him), and intrude on our family in our time of grief.

I also knew that such a man was unlikely to care one little bit about anyone or anything but himself and his own agenda so, of course, I said and did none of those things.

In the same businesslike voice, I simply replied that the matter was in the hands of our lawyers, and he would need to speak with them. Then I ended the call by hanging up. Enough was enough.

It wasn't the end, though. I then had to advise our lawyer of the phone call. He was adamant that the attempt to contact Jim should not have occurred and told us to continue to refer any future calls to him. There were no more calls and the other party withdrew their application the following January.

## Chapter Nine

## Our Kingdom Gone

*"Thankfully, this world is but a fleeting moment in Eternity, and what seems gone to us is only temporarily lost."*
*~ Anonymous*

Eventually, the funeral director called to let me know that William's body was now in their care and a time was arranged for me to go to the funeral home to see my baby again. I chose with care an outfit for William. As with all of my children, I had shopped for William's baby clothes and washed them all in advance. I packed a bag with singlet, nappy, clothes, bootees, hat, hairbrush, face washer, towel and bunny rugs ready to take for the first and only time I would bathe and dress my baby son.

I remembered the day I went shopping for boys' clothes for the first time at Chadstone a couple of months earlier. It had been a beautiful time, just me and William in my pregnant belly. I chatted to him as I strolled through the baby clothes section in David Jones, delightedly choosing grow suits with martians and cars on

150

them. After two girls, it was a novelty to be choosing blue bunny rugs and singlets.

Walking through the menswear section downstairs, my hands filled with shopping bags, I noticed a mother shopping with her son. The handsome, dark-haired young man looked to be in his late teens and stood over a head taller than his well-dressed mum. They smiled at each other and chatted easily as they shopped. My heart swelled with love for my own son moving inside my belly. I knew he'd be tall and somehow already knew that he would be handsome, dark haired and blue eyed. I'd imagined us shopping together here in the years ahead just like that mother and her son. Now, here I was, sitting on my bed with the clothes I had bought that day laid out before me, and these were the clothes my son would wear to his funeral and cremation.

I longed to hold him again and soon the day came when Sherrin picked me up to drive me out to the funeral home in Ringwood. Upon arrival, we were ushered into a peaceful room. The funeral director had already explained that William's appearance had changed, that there would be some deterioration of his skin and that he would be very cold. There was a baby bath prepared, ready for me to bathe my baby. Then we were left to spend this only opportunity for private time with William. I knew that it was okay to cry out and express my grief but I could not. William was my baby and I wanted to be present and focused on every precious moment with him, knowing that the time was soon coming when even his dead body would be lost to me forever.

Historically, it was often the women of a family who bathed and wrapped the bodies of their dead. It is only in relatively recent history that our society has become increasingly disconnected and distanced from death as a part of life. The ritual of bathing William's body, of caring for him and attending to his needs this one last time, was a way of honouring him and of preparing myself to farewell his soul's vehicle.

There was an incision on his torso that was stitched up. The funeral director did not know what it was when I questioned her and thought it must have occurred at the Coroner's. After so many days, it was obvious that William's spirit had long since departed from his body. His body, the precious vehicle that had briefly housed his spirit, was deteriorating. It was time for him to be laid to rest.

There are things about arranging a funeral for a baby that are unlike any other funeral. For starters, who do you invite? William did not know anyone. He never had the chance to open his eyes, make friends, meet his grandparents, go to school or go to work. Yet so many people, friends and family had been looking forward to meeting him. We did not want any strangers, acquaintances or fans turning up just because Jim was William's father, so we decided against any death notices in the newspaper. We simply printed a flyer with the funeral details and gave it to friends to distribute. I also sent the details to the private hospital and the Mercy.

There were flowers to be organised. The wonderful Highland dance community gathered close and supported us once again, this time in our grief. Holly's dance teacher poured all her love into creating beautiful floral arrangements and installed them at the chapel before the funeral.

I had nothing to wear that fit my post pregnancy body and did not want to wear maternity pants to William's funeral. My friend Judy, a school mum, picked me up and drove me to Chadstone to shop for clothes. It was the last thing I felt like doing and Judy knew it. So she arranged for a store shopper to take us to a spacious fitting room where I could sit whilst she brought clothes for me to try. The girls also needed suitable dresses, nothing too bright, and we walked to the children's-wear shop in the local High Street for those.

Then there was the music, something very important to us. Music has always been intrinsic to our lives, both personally and professionally. Jim had only one song request for William's funeral and that was his own signature song, 'Because I Love You', the soundtrack to his life. My throat closed and my heart ached as I looked at him. This song had been our bridal waltz and Jim always dedicated it to me when I was at his gigs saying, "This is for Karin, my beautiful wife." It was the final song in every live set that Jim performed, with crowds singing along joyously to the chorus, *Do what you wanna do, be what you wanna be, yeah*. Now, it would forever after be his final gift to William, William's song.

How could Jim ever sing it again without remembering? How could I ever hear it again without crying?

That left four more songs to be chosen for the service and I knew exactly what they would be. With some help from our friend Martin, who had created our website for Masters Apprentices, a CD was compiled.

The day of the funeral dawned. We arrived at the appointed time and were ushered into a private room where William awaited us. I sat down and William was handed to me, dressed in the outfit I had chosen and swaddled in a bunny rug. A tiny white coffin was in the room and I let my gaze slide away from it, focusing on my baby, trying to remember every last moment of this final time holding him in my arms.

Holly and Bonnie had already written a message for William to be read at his funeral. They had decorated it with drawings and it was to be placed in the coffin with William. Julie had also set up some lovely craft items for them to colour and decorate for William as we waited for friends and family to arrive.

I sat with William in my arms, holding him to my heart, whispering silently to his spirit. My parents and sister had arrived from the Gold Coast and came in to see their only grandson and nephew. I had not seen my sister in years and when I looked up and met her eyes, it was as though the years fell away. It was like looking at the face of love.

All too soon, we had to let William go for the final time. I don't know how I found the strength to do it silently. That scream inside me, the one that had been there from the time of William's death, was still there and threatened to erupt. I was getting used to it, though, and gulped it back down as William's tiny body was placed in the coffin and the lid was closed.

Tenderly, Jim picked up the tiny coffin and cradled William against his chest.

The poignant opening chords of 'Tears in Heaven', by Eric Clapton, began to play and the girls and I followed Jim and William up the centre aisle of the chapel. There seemed to be a lot of people standing to either side, but I remained focused on Jim and the heartbreakingly tiny coffin he carried to the altar. There, Jim gently laid Billy's coffin on the table, then walked over to sit beside us in the front row.

The funeral director began to speak, but my eyes were locked on Billy's coffin. Beside it was a framed photo of him along with a cross and candles glowing softly. A baby cried. Oh my God. My beautiful Billy had never made a sound. How could life be going on around his dead body? How could he be dead while another baby cried at his funeral? A guttural sob welled up in my throat and I could not hold it in. It came out and Holly shooshed me, looking alarmed. Clenching down on the next sob, I sat rigidly with tears pouring silently down my cheeks, the odd snuffle the only sound.

The time came for the part of the service where each person was invited to approach the altar and light a candle for William. Around 100 people were there to honour William and the three songs I'd chosen for this were all Jim's. Each song was chosen for its deeply personal meaning.

'Because I Love You' by Masters Apprentices
'The Only Ones' by Jim Keays
'Will Ye No' Come Back Again' by Jim Keays

'The Only Ones' was written by Jim as a love song to me and the lyrics are about his love for me and our family. "Will Ye No' Come Back Again" was written by Jim for his mother, Nancy, after her death some years earlier. It is a heartrending lament for the mother he never knew for most of his life. Jim had reworked the lyrics to a traditional Scottish song in her honour. Both songs were from a previously unreleased album which was recorded at Woodstock, Joe Camilleri's studio in East St Kilda.

As the last note faded, I sat gazing at the huge bowl of dancing flames, overwhelmed with love. Each and every person had walked up to light their candle for William, then turned around and looked at me with tears shining in their eyes as they returned to their seats. Some paused and bowed their heads to me, some blew kisses. Family, friends, neighbours, business owners from our local shopping strip, all had turned up to pay their respects to William and show their support for our family. William would have had a wonderful life with so many caring people around us.

I had watched in gratitude as William's paediatrician from the Mercy lit his candle for William. Some of the nurses from the private hospital also attended. Then I watched with a certain numbness as the obstetrician approached William's coffin and lit a candle. I wondered what he was feeling.

Before long, the service was drawing to its conclusion. Once again, for the last time, Jim walked over to pick up Billy's little coffin with reverence. The girls and I followed as we walked back down the aisle to the voice of my beloved Rod Stewart singing 'Forever Young'. Rod Stewart, my idol and musical hero from the age of thirteen, had provided the soundtrack to my life. Rod's beautiful song was my parting gift to my son. It felt like a benediction.

There was no wake. No celebration of life and sharing of memories of a life well-lived. Baby William, in his coffin, was placed in the back of a funeral director's sedan to be taken to the crematorium. Following the car to the crematorium was not an option given to us. We were told that the babies were cremated last, at the end of the day. There really is nothing at all that is 'right' about the death of a baby.

We went back to our home for a cup of tea with my family and a few close friends. Although I held it together, I was desperate to collapse and give way to the grief clawing at my insides.

*

William's NICU paediatrician had stayed in touch with us and had urged Jim and me to get away with the girls for a few days after the funeral, so we booked ahead at a guest house on Phillip Island. The next morning, we packed the car and left. Sitting in the front passenger seat, tears began pouring silently down my face. It was as though the well of grief inside me had sprung a slow leak and it could not be stopped. I spoke normally when required to, did what needed to be done as a wife and mother, all on autopilot, but the silent tears continued to spring afresh in between. When we walked to the beach at Cowes, I put a towel on the grass in the shade of a tree and immediately laid down and cried. Jim took Holly and Bonnie down to the water and they built castles and mermaids in the sand. I remember lying there on my side crying. Through eyelids that were almost swollen shut, I saw two women sitting a few metres away watching me. I didn't care, could not stop and did not want to. Just closed my eyes again and continued to cry.

That afternoon I noticed that the girls had yet another dose of the head lice that was running rampant through Holly's school. Holly had glorious long blonde ringlets that seemed to be a magnet for the bloodsuckers, probably because their eggs were almost impossible to see in her hair. Delousing is one of my least favourite things in life. Jim went down to the chemist in Cowes to pick up some treatment and I sat behind the girls, fine-combing their tea-tree soaked hair, weeping silently all the while. Those four days in Philip Island were some of the most miserable days of my life.

Oddly enough, the girls have many good memories of that time, which is exactly what we'd hoped for.

*

Back in Melbourne, life resumed on a bewildered sort of autopilot. William's ashes were personally delivered to our home by the funeral director. The box was heartbreakingly small and it immediately became precious beyond compare. I wanted to find a beautiful piece of furniture to hold William's ashes and all his things. Because what do you do with all the lovingly washed, ironed and labelled clothes for a baby who died? What do you do with all the special gifts that were given to us by family and friends in anticipation of his arrival? The photos, videos and mementos of his funeral? I wanted to cherish everything to do with William, so we were looking around for the right piece, which was proving difficult to find.

My 39th birthday in early December coincided with the first night of the Cotton Keays & Morris' three-week acoustic residency at Capers, a now defunct venue in Hawthorn, five nights a week. So Jim took us to the movies on the night before and bought a cake and my favourite Armani perfume for the morning of my birthday.

Sam, my beloved father-in-law had booked to fly from the UK to spend the Christmas period with us and meet his new grandson, and was due to arrive on 4 December. When William died, Sam asked if we would like him to postpone the holiday, but we wanted him here as much as he wanted to be with us. His life without Nancy had been increasingly solitary since her death. We all loved Sam dearly and looked forward to having him with us over Christmas.

Jim could not pick Sam up from the airport due to the CKM residency, nor could I as I still wasn't allowed to drive after the caesarean. I booked a chauffeur to collect Sam at the airport and drive him straight to our home in the eastern suburbs.

It was great having Sam with us and he loved our home, but most of all, he loved us and we loved him. Sam loved to walk for miles and would set out each day with his Akubra hat on, given to him by Jim years earlier, to explore the area. He also enjoyed a pint at the pub, but we lived in the middle of Melbourne's only remaining designated dry zone, a curious relic left over from the Prohibition era of the 1920s. Not one to be deterred, Sam returned home one hot summer's day, reporting that he had found a pub with beer on tap! Turns out, he'd walked all the way to the Matthew Flinders Hotel and back, a minimum five-kilometre round trip involving a pretty big hill. Thereafter, Sam's daily walks inevitably saw him call in to the Matthew Flinders for lunch and a pint.

I thought I was doing a good job of keeping the home life normal in the lead-up to Christmas. We rented a cabin in Daylesford for the annual Highland gathering. Holly was competing in the Highland dancing competition and we thought it would be nice for the whole family to get away for the weekend in beautiful Daylesford. I put on a brave face to ensure that everyone had a good time.

Back at home, the kindness of friends and neighbours meant that I never had to worry about her being picked up and dropped back home whilst I recovered from surgery. I attended school assembly to see Holly accept an award and packed a picnic basket for the school end-of-year outdoor event. The Christmas tree went up and the house was decorated.

Some things, though, you just don't see coming. The school Christmas service was to be held at a church very near our home. Holly had a part in the nativity play and I strolled up to watch, taking a seat on one side of the church. The children were seated in the middle, some in biblical costume, and a nativity scene was set up at the front. The service began with hymns and a sermon about Christmas before the nativity play commenced. It was during the sermon that it dawned on me that Christmas was all about the birth of a baby boy. Now, this may seem to be stating the bleeding obvious, but to the freshly bereaved mother of a baby boy, the realisation hit like a tonne of bricks leaving me stricken and paralysed with grief. The scene before me receded and I was back in the hospital theatre with William, feeling the pushing and shoving as his lifeless body was lifted out of mine, the words of the obstetrician and William's tiny body on the trolley beside me being breathed for by the anaesthetist through a tube. I was in church, but it felt like I was in hell. My eyes refocused and met the gaze of a female teacher across the room. Her eyes bored into mine and she looked like she was crying, willing me to see that she understood. I lowered my gaze and waited torturously for the service to end. I couldn't get out of there quick enough.

\*

Soon after I was referred to a psychologist for grief counselling and it was there that I learned about situational memory and how to anticipate situations that may trigger traumatic memories. The nativity scene at church was definitely one of them. This was just one of the effects of my grief and trauma.

My brain functions were also completely different. It felt like the neurological pathways had been shaken up and scrambled so violently that it took a long time to remember ordinary, everyday things. However, I had no trouble at all recalling every aspect and moment of the trauma that caused the grief – the trauma of William's induction, labour, birth and death. In fact, those things consumed my mind. My brain was so filled with the images, thoughts and memories of what happened that there was no room left for the minutiae of life.

Outwardly I think I appeared, well, normal. Inside was a whole other world. Part of my mind was always there, back in the days, hours and minutes of the artificial induction of labour, of William's birth and his death.

I would forget names, people, faces, events that I never did before. Often, when confronted with people I knew I should know, and sometimes know well, my mind would completely fail to recall who they were. I occasionally confused them with other people, calling them by the wrong name. The more this happened, the more I doubted my own ability to recall names and faces accurately. It got to the point that, even if I knew a person's name, I was too scared to use it because I feared I might have it wrong.

Every single moment of William's birth and death was etched in my memory and on constant replay in my mind, crystal clear, and there was little room in my mind for anything else.

Myriad questions started to mull over and over in my mind, my subconscious slowly sorting through what had occurred, always having the feeling that the answer to something crucially important was just around the corner. I needed to understand what had happened to William in order to be at peace with it. I attached no blame to anyone as I still chose to believe that everyone had done their best under tragic circumstances. I felt I needed to understand in order to forgive, if indeed forgiveness was necessary but didn't know how to find the answers to my questions.

A friend quietly suggested I call and ask the coroner, which I did. I was told to obtain my medical records but hesitated to do so, not wanting to cause any distress to those people involved in William's birth. To my mind, they must have been feeling their own grief over their part in William's death and I did not want to cause any more.

Things weren't adding up. I felt like I was living a double life, keeping everything running in the Keays household on the outside, whilst inside, my mind was mulling over questions like a forensic detective.

I made an appointment to see the obstetrician and also rang the hospital to request my medical records, thinking that these should provide the answers to many of my questions.

It became immediately apparent that seeing one's own medical records was not as easy and straightforward as it should be. I was told that my request should be put in writing to the Director of Nursing, who was currently on leave. Nobody else could process the request. Once the DON returned, the records would then need to go to the hospital's legal department before they could be released.

I felt like I was being given the runaround. Until that moment, I had deliberately and consciously cultivated the spirit of loving forgiveness around whatever had occurred, but this was like a slap in the face. There was no care for William or myself being shown here. My medical records and William's records were personal and should, in my opinion, have been immediately available to me upon request. The response I received made it clear to me that they considered our records to be the property of the hospital and that I would only get to see what their legal team allowed me to see.

The blinkers fell away and I woke up right then and there. I was overcome with a sickening feeling of dread, that in trying to do the right thing by everyone involved, I had given them a five-week head start to get working on their legal defence. Whilst I'd been all spiritual and focused on understanding, they had been all about business and damage control. I felt stupid and gullible, then fury flared within me for the first time and quickly settled into a slow burn that would be with me for years to come.

Any healing period, if there was one, evaporated once I woke up to the fact that it would not be easy to get answers to my questions about William's death. I shied away from what I now realised would be a David against Goliath fight if I continued to ask for answers to my questions. I didn't want a fight, I wanted to heal. Heal my grief, heal my family's grief, heal our life. December was busy enough with the lead-up to Christmas without the added stress of the imminent meetings I'd booked with my GP, the paediatrician and the obstetrician along with a representative from the hospital. Hoping they would answer my questions, I held off writing the official request for medical records.

On that same day, 8 December, I received a letter from the Victorian Forensic Institute informing me that a plaster cast of William's footprints had been taken while he was there, and it was now ready for collection. I had no idea that this had been done!! My heart raced and my throat constricted. Tears streamed down my face as I jumped in the car and raced down the freeway to South Melbourne to collect this most precious and unexpected gift.

Back in the car, I unwrapped the package with shaking hands. Mounted on a wooden shield, William's beautiful baby feet were painted in bronze with a small plaque beneath. Engraved on the plaque was his name and date of birth. Tears rolled unchecked as I gently traced his tiny toes and feet with my fingertips – carefully, so as not to get them wet. Those were very long feet for a newborn baby. He had my feet! My son would definitely have grown up to be a tall man.

The following day saw us front and centre at The Wiggles concert thanks to our wonderful friend Dianna O'Neill. Dianna had worked with The Wiggles and told them about William. The Field brothers understood all too well the tragedy of losing a child as Paul's daughter had died of SIDS. We were graciously invited to meet The Wiggles and cast before the show and the kindness and compassion shown to our family will never be forgotten. This day was a small but lovely reprieve from the hell we were living in.

*

That telephone call to request my medical records prompted the head of midwifery at the private hospital to arrange a meeting with me at our home the day after the Wiggles concert. I had prepared several questions that had been bothering me. She admitted to being unable to answer my questions regarding the timing of events as there was no time recorded on the CTG trace. I was told that the time should have been on the CTG printout, but no reason was given as to why it was not.

When I asked what time the records state that the obstetrician was contacted about William's abnormal heart rate, I was told that there were no records from 3:00 pm as the midwife stopped writing things down when she first became concerned and that, in such circumstances, the midwives would stay with the patient instead of writing records. She suggested I put my questions to the obstetrician at the six-week checkup.

Jim came with me to the see the obstetrician for my routine six-week post-birth check-up, where I asked the same questions that I had put to the head of midwifery. I had four simple questions. The first was regarding the time he was contacted by the hospital. He had no idea. With each question he became more defensive. I had tried to keep an open and forgiving heart, but it was clear that nobody wanted to look closely and learn from William's death.

At both meetings, first with the head of midwifery then with the obstetrician, the answers were either unclear or differed from each other in the crucial aspect of times. The obstetrician maintained that there was nothing to indicate that the situation was an emergency. Clearly, it was an emergency of the highest order considering the outcome.

The obstetrician had a copy of a CTG trace and asserted that the CTG ran at 1 cm per minute. Working backwards from the approximate time that he said I was taken to theatre, he presented a very vague and confusing explanation, the essence of which was that there was no window of opportunity to save William.

The next day, I mailed a letter to the Director of Nursing requesting copies of all medical records be forwarded to me as soon as possible. Two days later, I received a phone call from our obstetrician, who sounded upset and nervous. He wanted to arrange a time to meet with Jim and me along with a hospital representative. He said that he felt that our questions had not been answered satisfactorily and that he had gone over my hospital records several times in the days since our meeting in an attempt to work out the timing of the events leading up to William's birth. This is something that I believe should have been done six weeks earlier, considering that William died as a result. We agreed to meet with them at our home, after Christmas.

*

By day, I was managing the home office, the children, shopping for Christmas presents and planning for Christmas Day. Christmas was to be held at our house this year and there would be ten people. Sherrin and I took it in turns to host Christmas and we shared the cooking of a traditional roast lunch. Canapes, non-alcoholic fruit punch, turkey, ham, chicken, beef, cauliflower cheese, roast vegetables, greens, gravy, Christmas pudding, pavlova and trifle!

Jim was working five nights a week and taking it easy during the day as a result, conserving his energy for the next night's gig. In retrospect, I can see that everyone expected too much from me, too soon. No-one more so than I.

Beneath the veneer of the capable woman trying to keep everything 'normal' was a traumatised, grief-stricken mother whose arms ached to hold her baby and whose heart felt like a bloody, oozing, lacerated lump of agony. Each time I had to function in the outside world, I imagined slapping an adhesive bandage on it. The heart kept bleeding through the bandages, so I just kept slapping more on top. That is how I felt inside whilst all the time feeling there was a door, just there, if only I could make my eyes see it. The closest description of this is like the scene in *Gladiator*, when Russell Crowe's character dies, he sees a door in another dimension – the door to his heart's desire, to his family and LOVE.

I felt that door and searched for it constantly, between two worlds, not fully in this one, my soul sensing the next one tantalisingly close. I could feel it, feel the vibration of it and this sort of half-life was the shadow world I existed in until the day of the punchbowl incident.

It cracked me out of my shadow world and snapped me straight back into this one – and this reality was not one of cupcakes and fairy floss. No, it involved one of my children climbing the shelves of a cupboard and causing it to collapse, smashing the glasses of the punchbowl set just before Christmas. Sam had cleaned up the mess as best he could, but restacking the contents of the shelves had been left for me.

As ridiculous as it sounds, it was the circuit breaker and, just like that, I snapped. I did not want to be in this world. I no longer wanted to deal with the broken glass of life, nor did I feel able to. I wanted to be with William. Without saying a word, without conscious thought, I grabbed my keys, turned my back on the mayhem and sprinted to the car, driving blindly through traffic all the way, heading instinctively for the beach.

I drove down to Rickett's Point, a family favourite where we had spent many happy hours in the café and on the sand. Everyone except William, a sweet innocent baby who would never know the delight of beach and waves and sunshine and sandcastles. Sweet William, who never opened his eyes and who now lay in ashes in a tiny box in the bedroom.

The day was overcast. I was fully clothed in long, black pants and the grey blue water stretched out before me. Could I do it? Could I swim out there until I was tired enough to just let the water take me? It wasn't that I wanted to die, so much as I wanted to be with my baby more than I wanted to be here.

Almost running, my legs hit the water and I lunged like a woman possessed thigh-deep into the water, fully clothed, right along the beach until a natural rock barrier barred my way. I turned, sobbing mindlessly, and waded the length of the beach to the rock pools at the other end. There was no thought, no intention. Just misery. My mind had shut down.

Walking barefoot over the rocks, I sat on the edge, dangling my feet in the water. Time warped and suspended, and I sat crying, waiting. Waiting for the way to be shown. Maybe, if I sat there long enough, the darkness would descend, the tide would come in and I would float away.

My mind was frozen. It was as if I had left my body and my soul was hovering just above my shoulder, not quite in me, yet not quite gone. Sitting there perfectly still, at last, I felt peace. There was nothing else I had to do other than just sit there exactly as I was.

To this day, I have no idea how long I sat there in that out-of-time-and-body place until softly, softly and ever so gently the tiniest sensation drew my attention. From eyes that were mine, yet not, I looked down into the water.

There was the cutest little crab nibbling gently and industriously away at my big toe! Remaining motionless, I gazed at this sweet little creature and the ghost of a smile moved through me. Perhaps, if I sat there long enough, I would be eaten by crabs! It was the slightest twinge of dark humour, but it was enough to bring me slowly back into my body.

I sighed and looked at the little guy tickling my toe. Divine helpers come in all shapes and sizes and there is no doubt in my mind that this creature was sent to get me to wake up to myself. I moved my toe a fraction and he sat back a little before scuttling away. Pain, anguish and desolation crashed through me once again. The air was cold, the water was cold and I was freezing.

Still, I continued to sit there and let my mind acknowledge the stark reality that had to be faced. Even if I died and was blessed enough to be with William, my daughters would still be here and equally as unreachable to me as William was now. Holly and Bonnie were here with me in this life and needed their mother. There was no winning in this scenario. No happy outcome for me. Who was to say that I would be reunited with William after death anyway?

I heaved a great sigh again and stiffly, painfully, clambered up from the water, making my way back to the beach. Time to go home and look after my family. They would be worried. And Sam was there, darling Sam, still living with his own grief of losing his beloved Nancy.

A life of heartache, yearning and desolation stretched out before me, but it was my life, to be lived out until my time to die came of its own accord. All I could do was live my life in the best way I could and pray that it would be enough to let me be with William at the end of it.

## Chapter Ten

# Love Is

*"Think for yourself or others will think for you,
without thinking of you."*
~ Henry David Thoreau

Christmas came and went. The joy and laughter of the holiday season did not come naturally despite our best efforts to make good memories for the girls, but 2003 was not done with us yet. The meeting that Jim and I had asked for with the obstetrician and head of widwifery was set for 29 December.

They arrived at our house with a thick folder that was apparently my hospital file, copies of which I had yet to receive. The obstetrician produced two original CTG printouts: the first, he said, was done on my admission to the private hospital at 9:00 am and the second, he said, commenced at 3:45 pm. When I asked them where the other CTG scans were, they asserted that there were no other scans. When they showed us other sections of the records with entries after 3:00 pm, I wasn't having a bar of it.

I had already been told at a previous meeting with the head of midwifery that there was nothing written in the records after 3:00 pm as that was when the midwife had first become concerned, and at such times, nurses would stay with the patient. This made sense. The only problem with this explanation was that the midwife was definitely not with us the whole time.

By this time, I was so upset by the contradictory information that I didn't know what to believe and could hardly wait to get them out of my house. I ended the meeting by telling them that I still did not understand why William had to die.

After they left, for us, nothing had changed. We felt that an emergency situation had occurred as a result of me being artificially induced at the direction of our obstetrician, and that I had not been adequately monitored. To us, he was not there when he was needed.

Our son had died, and meetings with those involved raised even more questions rather than answers. A version of events was being presented to us that was very different from the reality we had experienced. And more concerning, that version had changed with each meeting. It felt like we were being gaslighted.

An appointment with our GP soon after didn't help. I thought our trusted family doctor would at least listen to my concerns and perhaps offer some advice. Instead, the first response was to look alarmed and begin writing a prescription for antidepressants, which I flatly refused. Dulling my memories and emotions by masking my grief with drugs would not help me heal but merely delay the process. I was there to discuss my concerns with a trusted medical professional about my son's death, not be given antidepressants.

It felt like the medical world was closing ranks on me, a feeling that I would experience repeatedly in the years ahead. Another friend, a nurse, had warned me that the medical industry would fight me at every step in my search for the truth. She warned that they would try to sweep the whole thing under the carpet and make it go away. She went on to say that, if pushed, they would try to put the blame on me and, if that didn't work, the blame would be shifted to the nursing staff. In the end, that is exactly what would happen, but it would be years before I knew that.

I knew now that I was going to have to write to the coroner if I wanted answers, yet still I hesitated. The obstetrician was a close friend of our neighbours and we lived in the same community, as did many of the hospital staff. Holly went to school with some of their children. With Jim's public profile, I always tried to protect our privacy wherever possible. A public inquest would mean our private family life would be open to scrutiny.

When I finally obtained my medical records, it looked like the sheaf of poorly photocopied pages had been thrown in the air, dropped on the ground and mixed up before being haphazardly put together again. Nothing was in sequence, the copied pages of the CTG trace were mixed in amongst other pages of notes and records. I'd never read medical records before, and didn't know what they should look like, but I didn't think they'd look like this.

The CTG trace was an unintelligible graph of squiggly lines. I didn't know how to read it and had to teach myself. When I finally did, I cried for days. In my search for answers, I would study this trace repeatedly in the years to come and cry every time I had to refer to it. What had initially looked like a lot of squiggly lines was the physical record of my baby son's asphyxiation and decline into death. I still cannot look at it without crying.

There was a lot of information, yet no obvious answers. It felt like I was fumbling in the dark with little understanding of the medical records. One night, after the girls were in bed, I took a deep breath and began to put the pages of records into order. Laying them all out on the dining room table and floor, I set about putting the puzzle pieces together.

I began to write, jotting questions and notes into a notepad that filled up fast. I was a recently bereaved mother, writing from that perspective. There was no indication yet that my request for a coronial investigation would be granted. I was simply hoping for answers to my questions. I had no idea that my initial letters would later be used as my witness statement in court when an inquest was eventually called. I was told by the coroner's office to put my questions in writing along with as much detail of the events as I could remember. That is what I did.

The medical people involved would write their statements knowing that they were writing a legal statement. Undoubtedly, they would have been written either in conjunction with their lawyers, or at least reviewed by their lawyers before submission.

*Mr. Graeme Johnstone*
*State coroner*

*Dear Mr. Johnstone,*

*Reference is made to coroner's case number 3683/03 for my son, William Grant Keays.*

So began the first of many letters over the coming years, all commencing with those same words. By day, I kept our family and business life as normal as possible. In the evenings, after Holly and Bonnie were asleep, I pulled out the medical records and notepad and began to write on behalf of our son. William could not speak for himself and nobody other than I would do this for him. Moving on and putting his death in the past was not an option. Anytime it was suggested to me that the toll of taking on the medical establishment might be too much to bear, I would answer that it was not only about William. What if the same thing happened to another baby? What if it were my own grandchild? How could I live with that and how would my daughters ever forgive me for not trying to ensure it never happened again?

My first letter to the coroner began to take shape. With so many questions and so much information, I broke it down into four sections: a cover letter, my recollection of events on and around

William's birth, a list of twelve questions and concerns, and a history of my pregnancies and births.

Some of the questions centred on the obstetrician's reasons for induction and his behaviour and actions on the day. I asked the coroner why it took so long for the obstetrician to get there. I asked what was the truth about the time that the obstetrician was contacted. At our meeting, he said people had to move cars at his house. He gave this as a reason why he was delayed. I asked the coroner if he was entertaining that afternoon. I asked if alcohol was involved.

I raised my concerns about an article I read in the financial pages of the newspaper whilst I was pregnant, which reported that a large corporation was selling off its private hospitals (of which this private hospital was one) to concentrate on its other interests. Could this have contributed to the level of care that William and I received and the subsequent lack of clarity around the timing of events? The corporation ownership would have had a lot to lose from any negative publicity and staff may have worried about their job security.

I raised my concerns over the accuracy of the medical records. Given that no records were kept after 3:00 pm, as we were told at our first meeting with the head of midwifery, I believe that the obstetrician's and hospital's version of the timing of events were guesstimated and filled in retrospectively, knowing that William had died, to reduce the amount of recorded time that William was in distress without a doctor in attendance.

The letter was prepared, but I held off sending it until after the Christmas/New Year holiday period. I didn't want it sitting at the bottom of someone's inbox. Deep down, I was also fearful of what might lay ahead once I publicly challenged the medical system. Since William's death, friends had contacted me at various times to tell me stories of other mothers whose babies had died before, during or after childbirth. These were stories of women, some of whom I knew, yet I had no idea they had been through the same devastating loss. Each of these stories was whispered in confidence, the details sketchy. The mothers either could not or would not speak with me themselves for fear of legal repercussions. At that time, I did not understand what this meant.

My heart ached for them, but it also burned with a sense of betrayal. If babies were dying and the parents weren't speaking out about issues within the medical system, the issues would not change. Babies would continue to die and maybe, had someone spoken up, William might not have died. Perhaps those parents had not been able to function in their grief. God knows, only two months into my own grief, I was barely keeping it all together. Whatever way I looked at it, it was up to me to do something. I could not live with myself if another baby died and I could have prevented it.

Then came the day when I received a phone call from Lisa, the same friend and neighbour who had looked after the girls during William's birth and death. A mutual friend and school mum had called Lisa to ask if I would be open to speaking with her about

William's birth. Her sister, Karyn, had just lost her baby during delivery at the same hospital as I. The same midwife was in attendance and synthetic oxytocin was used.

The baby's name was Saoirse Grace Kennedy and she was born on 4 January 2004 but did not survive her delivery.

It felt like the earth had opened and I was freefalling into an abyss. Did this happen because I had procrastinated over the letter to the coroner? Could I have prevented it? *What* was going on over there? Grief, horror, disbelief, anger – the maelstrom of internal turmoil threatened to suck me down into oblivion. Karyn was not yet up for speaking with me, but I spoke with her sister and was given enough information to refer to Saoirse's death in my letter.

The similarities between the deaths of William and Saoirse after the turning on of synthetic oxytocin were extremely concerning to me. With William, the obstetrician came in and turned on the drug in the face of William's 'non-reassuring' CTG trace. This was done on a Saturday afternoon, in a private hospital, where there was no guarantee of an anaesthetist or theatre staff being on hand. In such circumstances, I question how an emergency caesarean could have been performed within 30 minutes, should it become necessary. Yet turning on the syntocinon was the first thing he did when he came in. You can see the immediate results on the CTG. The graph showing William's heartrate plummets and William fights for his life for the rest of the trace. Out of all the expert witnesses from RANZCOG (the Royal Australian and New Zealand College of Obstetricians and Gynaecologists) who provided opinions for the inquest, not one of them was critical of the obstetrician's actions on the day. This suggests that those actions were within the bounds of accepted standard obstetric practice in Australia.

Karyn Kennedy had gone into labour at 41+ weeks gestation and presented at the same private hospital two months and three days after William was born.

Synthetic oxytocin was administered and baby Saoirse gave an almighty thump in Karyn's tummy, then dropped off the CTG trace. The midwife was the same one who had attended me. Her obstetrician had just left the hospital but was still in the carpark. There were no anaesthetist or theatre staff present and they had to be called in, just as they had with William. Karyn was given an emergency caesarean some 45 minutes later, but Saoirse was unable to be revived and therefore was declared stillborn. After printing out the letter to the coroner, I signed it and mailed it straight away.

*

Strangely, life went on. Cotton Keays & Morris had their annual Zoo Twilights gig at Royal Melbourne Zoo on 9 January. Everybody loved a Zoo Twilights gig, especially the kids, and they were always packed. The stage was in the rotunda and the crowd set up their picnic rugs and chairs around it, a sea of happy faces stretching off into the distance. This year, several of our neighbours had bought family tickets and we set up our picnics together. Sam was with us and absolutely loved sitting in the camping chair, beer in hand, chatting with our friends in his delightful Scottish brogue. The lions roared in the background, and I wondered what they thought of the music. We got there early enough for the kids to wander off in a large group to see the animals while the adults relaxed before the show. The letter to the coroner had been sent and there was nothing more I could do for the moment. If my thoughts wandered at times from the beautiful summer evening, I was already learning to redirect them back to the present moment.

Sam flew back to the UK two days later and Holly started in Grade 3 at the end of January. There were meetings with the school to discuss how Holly could be supported, both academically and emotionally. The focus of concern tends to be on the mother; however, grief affects siblings in ways that are not always obvious and are often delayed. I was mindful of trying to keep family life running as normally as possible for the girls and shielded them from my activities around the coronial investigation. I'd pretty much settled into a routine of writing and researching until late into the night, after they were asleep. I kept my tears for that time, too. Years later, Holly told me that she would sometimes wake at night and hear me crying in the bedroom. Taking her doona and pillow, my darling little girl would make up a bed on the floor outside my closed door, so she could be near me. I never knew and it broke my heart all over again to hear it years later. No matter how hard I tried to shield them, our daughters' lives were shattered by William's death, too. Did I do the right thing by trying to protect them from my grief? I don't know. I know only that I did the very best I could with no books to read on the subject and no useful advice on how to parent my girls through the trauma and loss of our baby and their baby brother.

The various foundations built around baby and child death had booklets that were generalised and aimed at stillbirths and SIDS families. Not one of them wanted to discuss my baby's death by what I euphemistically called medical error. That is because, like cancer foundations, they work symbiotically with the medical industry to raise money for 'awareness', but, in my personal experience, cancer patients and their families do not benefit from people being 'aware'. The funds raised cover the salaries and expenses of the foundations, with any surplus being allocated to their chosen medical sector, usually promoted as going towards research.

Jim and I were conscious of nurturing our love for each other, so we made a point of making some time for just the two of us, for romance. It felt strange, almost forced, lacking the fun and spontaneity of our life before William, but we were both committed to our love and marriage. We knew we had to find our way through the grief and loss together, always turning towards each other, remembering that William was born of our love. In February, we went to the gorgeous art deco Rivoli Cinemas in

Camberwell to see *Lord of the Rings, Return of the King* on the big screen. On Valentine's Day, Jim's gift to me was a beautiful armoire from a home shop in Camberwell. Denny and Chris, the owners, were so lovely and, after hearing our story, went to great lengths to help us get the perfect piece to hold William's things, including his ashes.

Jim was producing a DVD documentary on Masters Apprentices and busy working on compiling footage, photos and filming interviews. The documentary would be called *Fully Qualified* and, like every aspect of the project, the concept was created entirely from Jim's vision and made reality through his lifetime of knowledge, experience and drive. My husband was an absolute professional in his chosen career, having worked constantly in the music and entertainment business since Masters Apprentices formed in 1965. He was the only member to have remained in the original band throughout its lifespan from 1965–2014. Not only the singer and co-writer of the band's biggest hit songs, it was also Jim's vision that served as the steadying rudder throughout. After the loss of the original 1965 lineup early on, it was generally accepted that Masters Apprentices was Jim's band and that there was no Masters Apprentices without Jim Keays.

Meanwhile, the Cotton Keays & Morris juggernaut was already booking corporate gigs into October, November and December, and it was still only March! With a fast-filling schedule of gigs, 2004 was shaping up to be a very busy year.

The coroner had issued an Advice for Statements early in 2004, which required the parties involved in William's investigation to provide statements. It also outlined the issues to be explored. In retrospect, I see clearly how I was always on the back foot, how the obstetrician and a well-practised medico-legal system were streets ahead, building their case to present a version of events very different from my own.

The Advice for Statements, three months after William's death, was when I first found out that the obstetrician had recorded that the labour was induced because of 'maternal discomfort'. Despite us so reluctantly agreeing to induction after it was presented to us as being for William's health and safety, there was no mention in his statement of possible shoulder dystocia or any potential issue with William. Simply, the medical records state the obstetrician induced me because he said I was uncomfortable. We had misplaced our trust in the obstetrician, and to us, his notes in my medical records confirmed why we had. Not only was there no reference to the potential issues that he had used to convince us to agree to the induction, in stating 'maternal discomfort' as reason for induction he had put the onus on me.

Before William's death, my only reference for childbearing loss had been the heart-rending death of Madeline Shepherd. Her parents, Sahara Herald and Brad Shepherd, were also in the music industry. Sahara has for many years been tour director for Frontier Touring, but back then she was the national event coordinator for Big Day Out. Brad is the guitar hero/songwriter in the Hoodoo

Gurus, another legendary Australian band also in the ARIA Hall of Fame. We'd celebrated with Sahara and Brad at their wedding and had been excited and delighted to hear that they were expecting their first child. Jim stayed in touch with Brad and had the due date marked in the diary. We hadn't heard anything, so I told Jim to give Brad a call. We were excited. I remember Jim asking jovially if they'd had the baby yet. I couldn't hear what Brad was saying, but I knew it wasn't good news. When Jim hung up, he was ashen. Their beautiful baby Madeline had died. We didn't know any details and it seemed intrusive to ask. I couldn't even begin to imagine how Sahara and Brad must be feeling, couldn't begin to imagine my own feelings if something had happened to Holly. I didn't know what to do. Sending a card seemed so trite, almost like an insult. Sending flowers seemed inappropriate. I imagined many people were calling her when the last thing she felt like was polite conversation. I didn't know what to do so I did nothing.

Time passed and with it the opportunity to reach out, or so I thought, but it felt like I had failed them somehow. I knew that my lack of response had probably not even been noticed. Grieving parents aren't counting cards or phone calls or flowers. They are just trying to breathe, to survive.

After William's death, I knew exactly what to do. I pulled out the box of gift cards of Jim's drawings that I'd commissioned from my friend, Liz, and wrote to Sahara and Brad. Finally, I found the words for the card I'd always wished I'd written after Maddie's death. I knew now that it was never too late, that I would not and could not upset Sahara by reminding her of her darling Maddie. Because mothers never forget their babies, they only learn to live with and hide their loss so that others aren't upset by their feelings. To hear a friend speak the name of their beloved child, to read their child's name on a card or letter, is to know that their child is remembered as a person and not forgotten. It is one of the greatest gifts you can give a mother.

Sahara called me as soon as she got the card. She hadn't known about William's death, but her empathy, kindness and obvious grief for me was palpable and immensely comforting. To hear her speak of our shared experiences was like a light in the dark.

\*

In mid-March, CKM were heading off to Sydney for another run of gigs, when Jim met up with the Hoodoo Gurus travelling back home from Melbourne on the plane. Jim called me as soon as he got to the hotel to tell me that he and Brad stood in the aisle of the plane, hugging and crying in shared grief for the loss of William and Madeline.

A few days later, Sahara flew into Melbourne and took a taxi to our home. We hugged, cried and talked and talked in ways that I couldn't with anyone else. We sat on the bed together and went through all William's things that were now in the armoire in our room. We went through all his photos, touched his things, while Sahara listened to my outpouring of feelings that I hadn't dared to share with anyone before, other than Jim. We talked about Maddie. Sahara had brought her own photos and we cried for beautiful Madeline. Sahara had brought a copy of a book for me to keep, a collection of short stories about childbearing loss, in which she shares her own story. The book is called, *Always a Part of Me. Surviving Childbearing Loss.* It was published by ABC Books in 2001 and was the best gift ever, right when I needed it most. In that book, Sahara explains how all the books she was given at the time of Maddie's death were of no great help to her. 'I had a big pile of books next to my bed, and it was the first time I'd ever actually opened the sections in the back on what happens if your baby dies. It's this really inane information that's completely useless.'

Sahara was close to her due date when she realised that she hadn't felt Maddie move that day. An ultrasound showed that Maddie had died in utero. Like me, Sahara was induced using synthetic oxytocin to give birth to her full-term baby; however, there was now no risk to Maddie that her oxygen supply would be cut off. I couldn't imagine how she and Brad must have felt, going through a full induced labour, knowing that their darling baby girl was already dead. Whilst initially thought to be a cord death, the pathology later revealed that Maddie had died from a condition called obstetric cholestasis, which causes the mother's liver to malfunction and release bile acid into the blood stream, crossing the placenta and potentially creating foetal heart failure if not detected in time. Liver function tests had previously been included in the suite of standard pre-natal tests covered by Medicare but had been excluded from the regular test protocol by the time of Sahara's pregnancy. If the condition had been detected by a simple blood test and monitored regularly it is highly likely that Maddie would have been delivered early and survived.

I remember Sahara telling me that her pregnancy had been extremely challenging, that she faced constant nausea and violent vomiting the entire time, right until the day Maddie died. Sahara described how she felt her body was in constant conflict with the baby, that there was an internal battle raging but that doctors and midwives were consistently dismissive of her concerns. Time and again, in many varied circumstances, I have heard of pregnant women's intuition and maternal instinct being overridden and ignored by medical personnel, to the detriment of their baby's health and even their life. I feel that when it comes to our baby's wellbeing, a pregnant woman's natural intuition is powerful and should be taken into careful consideration by obstetricians and parents alike.

## Chapter Eleven

## Broken Promises

*"If you want the present to be different
from the past, study the past."*
~ Baruch Spinoza

Daily life had been as busy for me as it was for Jim. I was organising quotes for gas fireplaces, shopping for marble surrounds and getting in soil for the garden. My diary was punctuated with times for the classroom help roster, Holly's funk dancing, play dates, and buying Easter cards and eggs. As always, there was bookkeeping, invoices to be paid and raised, taxes and wages to be done.

With life so busy and stressful, it had been easier to ignore the effects of the emergency caesarean on my body until now. There was a grapefruit sized lump in my abdomen. It protruded over the caesarean scar, which was so distressing to me that I never looked at my body in the mirror anymore. I could not bear to see the evidence of what had happened to me, the scars of stitches where the obstetrician had sliced open my belly and womb to pull

William's limp little body out. Not only had my son died, but I felt mutilated and I was left with a permanent macabre reminder of this. Although the lump itself did not hurt, I was experiencing abdominal pain. I'd seen a GP about it who said the pain should resolve with time. It didn't, it was getting worse.

An ultrasound of the area revealed no reason for the pain and I was referred to a general surgeon as I now had no gynaecologist and I had lost trust in any member of RANZCOG. An MRI also showed no reason for the pain and the lump was thought to be a possible incisional hernia. However, exhaustive ultrasounds failed to find any evidence of a hernia and the surgeon concluded it was probably muscle weakened by nerve damage. The surgeon's only other path was exploratory surgery, which I declined. It was suggested to me by more than one doctor that it may be in my head, a psychological response to the trauma. I already knew where that was headed. I have observed that when doctors can't find a diagnosis for pain, they often follow the bog-standard medical protocol and fall back on one of two prescription drugs: antidepressants or steroids. The protrusion became less noticeable as I lost weight and I resigned myself to living with the pain because I wasn't having more abdominal surgery just to take a look, nor would I be taking any psych drugs for a pain in my tummy that was very real.

Years down the track, it would be Kelly Ford to the rescue once again. In one of our catch-up phone calls, Kelly told me she was now working for an obstetrician and gynaecologist who, she assured me, was a lovely, kind man. She offered to speak with him and explain my circumstances to see if he was comfortable with taking me on as a patient. Shortly afterwards, Kelly called me back with an appointment time.

I fronted up for the appointment expecting to be looked upon as the enemy – after all, I was the woman who was daring to hold one of his college fellows accountable for the death of my son.

What I found was a genuinely kind and compassionate man who really wanted to help. When further scans showed no obvious reason for my abdominal pain, the doctor suggested a laparoscopy: keyhole surgery whereby a tiny camera would be inserted through my belly button so the doctor could have a look around to see what was causing my pain.

On the day Jim dropped me at the hospital, I remember wondering if this was the day that I'd get to see William again. I knew it wasn't serious surgery, but my most recent memories of going into hospital were not good ones. Whatever happened, I was at peace with it. To me, the worst-case scenario would be the doctor not finding any reason for the pain.

In the dreamy way of anaesthetic, I woke in recovery to find my doctor's kindly face hovering over me. He still had his surgical cap and mask on, and his eyes were so filled with empathy that they appeared to me to have tears in them.

Gently, with the utmost kindness, he explained to me what he had found. Scar tissue from the caesarean scar on my uterus had proliferated and grown out into my abdomen, coating my ovaries and fallopian tubes. The resultant squeezing of my ovaries and tubes was the cause of my pain. He had cut it all away and done his best to ensure that it never came back. My tummy was still scarred and misshapen on the outside but now, blessedly, free of pain. To this day, the pain has never returned, but, once again, it was purely by chance, by word of mouth from Kelly, that I found a doctor who would correctly diagnose and fix me.

\*

One day, CKM had an afternoon gig in Geelong at a great waterfront venue. I'd been to gigs there before and loved the vibe, so Jim suggested we make it a day out together. We arranged for a babysitter, and I picked Jim up from the airport, then we drove down to the gig. It was a lovely day for a road trip. This was one of the first times since William's death that I actually wanted to go out and have fun, instead of forcing myself to go. We did all the usual stuff that we loved doing together: chatting, listening to music, laughing, flirting, holding hands and, of course, stopping for a snack at the roadhouse. It was one of our traditions.

The gig was packed, and the room upstairs was, as always, filled with band members, their partners and friends. Most of them I knew, so there were a few greetings and catch-up chats to be had. The CKM banter wasn't just confined to the stage. The guys cracked jokes and took good-natured pot-shots at each other all the time.

So, I was a bit nonplussed when Russell turned to me and said, "You've done Jim a great disservice."

For a moment, I thought he was joking, but one look at his face showed he was serious. I couldn't begin to imagine why.

"What do you mean?" I asked.

"The guy that called to speak with Jim about the Trademark. He's the programmer for a radio network. Now he's furious and he's removed all Masters Apprentices songs from the play list and will never play them again on radio."

The penny dropped and I was transported back to the hellish nightmare of those days between William's death and his funeral, to the day I answered a phone call from a man wanting to speak with Jim about the Trademark. Was this the same man? The one who called our unlisted home number to speak about a matter that he knew was in the hands of our lawyer? Regardless of our recent family tragedy, he should not have been calling us anyway. My manner had been completely professional. He just hadn't got what he wanted when I referred him to our lawyer.

Tears welled in my eyes at the blatant unfairness of it all. Thankfully Russell changed the subject and it was the end of that conversation. I was still too fragile to deal with yet another issue that I felt was totally unfair. The boys went back to work and I stayed alone in the room, trying to stem the tears and regain my composure.

Masters Apprentices are in the ARIA Hall of Fame. Their songs have been on movie soundtracks, TV shows and advertising for decades, but how often do you hear them played on radio anymore? Other contemporaries of the band, Russell included, have their hits played regularly on radio, but it's been many years since I've heard the Masters unless it's on one of those Top 100 Greatest Australian Songs shows.

The fact that one person had the power to stop playing the songs of one of Australia's greatest bands, and was prepared to do it out of personal spite, I found appalling. It's the type of 'old boys' thinking that is gradually being eliminated from the Australian music industry, thanks to the professionalism and determination of some people, many of them women, who are paving the way for those who follow.

*

I'd noticed that Jim was looking tired and pale when he came home from work. Given the grief we lived with constantly and the added stress of lobbying for an inquest, it was little wonder. I gently suggested that he might like to have a general check up with a GP, just because he was in his mid-fifties and hadn't had one for a long time.

The Jim I married never went to the doctor, never took prescription drugs or any chemical drugs. He never touched alcohol unless he had a cold or sore throat, in which case he would gargle a shot of port before a gig, for his voice. He wouldn't even take a Panadol for a headache. If he wasn't feeling 100%, he would head out to visit his old friend Thommo to have his back put in and get some herbal remedy. Thommo was a naturopath and osteopath and Jim firmly believed that any aches and pains originated from the muscular skeletal system being out of alignment.

During the seventies, he'd eaten a macrobiotic diet, followed an energetic and spiritual guru, dressed according to colour therapy and read extensively on philosophy and spirituality. He'd even read the obscure, weighty tome of *The Urantia Book* from cover to cover.

It was Jim who taught me that today's Western medicine began as emergency medicine on the battlefields of the Crimean War. It wasn't about health and wellbeing, like for Eastern healers; it was about salvaging violently torn bodies. Jim had been told that in traditional Chinese medicine, which is a preventative medicine, it used to be that people would pay their doctors to keep them well and if they got sick, they didn't get paid. This is probably no longer the case, but it sounds logical to me.

So, I was mildly surprised when he agreed and asked me to book an appointment. Physically, Jim appeared to be fine, but the blood tests came back with a result that sent the doctor into panic mode. Jim's cholesterol level was 10.1. The doctor wanted him to go on statin drugs immediately, saying that high cholesterol was an indicator that can point to increased risk of heart attack and stroke. Jim was very aware that every drug has side effects, especially drugs that only mask symptoms and do not offer a cure.

Refusing to be panicked into making a fear-induced decision, Jim flatly refused the drug. He asked for more tests to see if there was any issue with his heart. An echocardiogram and stress test showed his heart was strong and healthy. Jim was told he had the heart of a 40 year old.

Despite the GP's dire prediction that lowering cholesterol naturally was very difficult to do, Jim went about modifying his diet and exercising. The results of his next blood test showed that his cholesterolwas lower but still very high. Jim kept doing what he was doing and the next one was down, almost to the high end of normal, and then the next test was even lower. The doctor was amazed. Jim mentioned, though, that the doctor said his iron levels were a bit low and that he needed to eat more red meat. Jim was still eating more than the recommended weekly amount of lean, red meat so we did wonder why his iron levels had fallen. I was proud of him for his commitment to his health and philosophy. The paleness never went away, though, and I put that down to the low iron, something he'd never had before. It would be another three years before we would come to realise that Jim's iron deficiency was a precursor to something far more devastating.

In August, 2004, our right to the Trademark of Masters Apprentices had been accepted, but that wasn't the end of the Trademark saga. By November, a huge corporate law firm had lodged a Notice of Opposition. We couldn't believe it. Why on earth would yet another lot of lawyers want to stop Jim from using the name of Masters Apprentices? They couldn't win. Jim's right to the name was indisputable, but, in the way of anything to do with the law, we would have to follow yet another stressful and extortionately expensive legal process through to the end. William's inquest had not yet begun, but we had already engaged our solicitor to ensure that we were properly represented. Now, he was handling the legal aspects of the inquest along with the second Trademark opposition.

As trivial as it may seem in comparison to the inquest and all that it involved, the drawn-out legal opposition to our application for the Trademark of Masters Apprentices continued throughout this time. Anyone who has ever been forced to deal with lawyers and legal battles will know all too well, that it is one of the most stressful things in life. In 2005, the instigators were forced to reveal themselves as one JMBP INC., production company of American TV producer Mark Burnett.

*The Apprentice*, with Donald Trump, was coming to Australia and it appeared that they were sending out their legal junkyard dogs in advance, indiscriminately laying waste to anything that might pose a threat.

Had JMBP or their lawyers bothered to ask us if we had any objection to them using the name, we would have said no. For a long while, we didn't even know who was objecting or why. When, finally, we received – through our own lawyer – a request to relinquish any claim to the name 'The Apprentice', we signed immediately. We knew they expected us to make a counteroffer, to at least try to recoup the many thousands of dollars their objection had cost us in legal fees, but we just wanted them to go away. It wasn't a path to prosperity that sat well with us.

We were grieving, traumatised parents, battling the medico-legal system for the truth of what had led to our son's death. We paid for the enormous legal costs in advance, by increasing our mortgage and drawing on the equity in our family home. Our quest was for social justice, not profit. Anyone who has held the body of their dead child would trade everything they own, in a heartbeat, to turn back time and have their healthy, whole child returned to life. As any parent who has survived their child knows, no amount of money can ever buy their heart's desire.

In October, William's first birthday was approaching and I planned to mark his birthday with a gathering that fell on the day before Melbourne Cup Day. I decided on a Cup Day inspired champagne and finger food buffet at our house. It was to be a relaxed affair and by way of a thank you to all the close friends who had really stepped up to support us through the last year. I busied myself planning the menu and ordering food, champagne, helium balloons and a cake from the shops in our local village. I wanted it to be lovely for our friends and also just in case our Billy could somehow visit us in spirit on his birthday, I wanted him to know how loved he was, that he would never be forgotten. It was everything I'd hoped it would be and I felt humbled by the love and care shown for William and our family that day and always.

By mid-November, I had my Christmas shopping list underway along with boots, thermals, hats and scarves for the girls' first experience of winter in the UK. We had booked our early bird airfares months ago and planned our itinerary. We looked forward to seeing Sam and couldn't wait to leave in early January, which was only weeks away.

Before long, we were out of Scorpio and in my sun sign of Sagittarius. Jim organised a surprise birthday dinner for my 40th at Circa, The Prince. It was my favourite restaurant at that time and we were joined at a big, round table by our closest friends for a beautiful evening of fine dining in St Kilda.

*

Still in Melbourne, my nightly routine of writing and research continued. On Boxing Day 2004, whilst most people were either celebrating or recovering, I was writing a nine-page letter to the coroner which was in two parts.

In Part 1, I requested that any investigation into William's death include a statement from Saoirse Kennedy's parents due to the same actions by some of the same people involved occurring.

Part 2 continued:

*Since my first letter to you, I have been in contact with Mrs Karyn Kennedy, who is the mother of Saoirse Grace Kennedy. Saoirse is the little girl referred to in my letter, who died during* labour (at the same private hospital) approximately two months after William. I understand that you will not investigate her case because Saoirse did not take a breath.

Whilst I realise that your office must draw the line somewhere, are you aware that there is no effective avenue for the independent investigation of stillborn babies?

Are you also aware that babies born with brain damage or ongoing problems as a result of mismanaged labour are known to result in high payouts from lawsuits because of the money needed to care for them?

Do you know that there is little or no consequence for a doctor or hospital as a result of a baby being stillborn?

However, the consequences of a child surviving a mismanaged labour with lifelong disabilities are far-reaching with major legal implications – read financial – for the doctors involved.

The points that I have raised are valid and extremely disturbing. They show a terrible loophole in the law related to obstetrics. There is a serious need for greater protection of unborn babies and I believe that laws regarding the conduct and accountability of obstetricians and private hospitals need urgent revision and sweeping changes.

Mr Johnstone, I see here an opportunity for a coronial investigation that has the potential to prevent the deaths of thousands of Australian children. Writing and researching this letter has been more difficult than I can adequately describe. I cannot look upon William's CTG trace without crying for hours *yet I have had to study it time and again in an effort to deduce what actually occurred. I would rather put my hand into a fire than go through the written records of William's birth and death, yet I have spent long hours poring over them time and again trying to piece things together. It is my fervent hope that you will now shoulder the burden of this knowledge that has been forced upon my husband and me and bring it out into the public spotlight so that in the future parents will be informed and not have to learn of it the way we did.*

The letter was signed, sealed and in the mail. I put it out of my mind and began the last-minute preparations for our holiday. The girls and I had never experienced winter in the Northern Hemisphere before and it was with much excitement that we boarded our long-haul flight only four days into 2005.

Our first stop was London. It was like a magical storybook with icy breath, twinkling lights and roasted chestnut vendors in the streets. We loved it.

Two days later, we were heading north in a hire car to spend a week with Sam. That was our first taste of just how ferocious the weather can be in England. A storm that lasted all night descended on Cumbria and was so violent that even I, a Queensland girl who grew up with cyclones, was a bit hypervigilant just in case the roof blew off! The next day, we drove through the village and saw trees down, houses with roofs missing and stone chimneys collapsed onto the streets. It didn't stop us from having fun with Sam, though, and English pubs in winter, with their open fires, are more charming than ever.

From there, we spent a few nights in the West country, dropping in for a cup of tea with Jim's friend Andy Scott from The Sweet.

We also spent a few nights in beautiful Amsterdam, which was eventful! Our friends Gypsy and Jeroen came to visit us at our historic hotel in the heart of town. We were all sitting in a café when Jim's wallet was pickpocketed whilst his jacket was draped over the back of his chair. The café owner spotted it happening and he and Jeroen gave chase down the lanes and cornered the thief, retrieving the wallet intact.

Back home in Melbourne, we hit the ground running and it was straight into business. Jim was hustling a TV show concept and there were plenty of bookings coming in. It was around this time that Glenn Wheatley called, asking Jim to submit a demo for the anthem of the newly formed Melbourne Victory football club. We instantly knew what the music would be. As keen footy and music fans, we'd often analysed the club songs, especially around the time that Jim wrote the lyrics for the Lions club song. In our scrutiny of the AFL club songs, I'd mentioned to Jim that there was one great old tune that had never been used and would make a cracker of a footy anthem – 'Scotland the Brave'.

When Glenn called, we looked at each other and knew Jim had a real chance against other submissions. Jim was working on the lyrics when I saw a news report on TV with the new Scottish coach for Victory being interviewed and called out to Jim to come and watch. One of the things he said was 'in the heat of battle' and I suggested that Jim jot it down because it's a great phrase and it would be fantastic to incorporate the coach's words. He did. The demo was recorded and submitted, and Glenn rang to say that Jim's song had been chosen, telling me, "Now Jim has two football anthems under his belt."

## Chapter Twelve

# Love in a Drugstore

*"Families can cope with the brutal truth; what they cannot handle are the lies and the cover-ups."*
~ Lorraine Long, Founder – Medical Error Action Group

The coroner's court inquisition upon the body of William Keays stretched over three years from 2006 to 2008, and is a true story with enough legal drama, plot twists and stunning revelations to make a stand-alone movie script. One with an awesome, readymade soundtrack. The two years prior were filled with research and lobbying and when the coroner handed down her finding in 2008, it had been nearly five years since William's death. The total legal fees, expert witness fees and associated costs to our family exceeded $80,000 and we increased the mortgage on our home to pay these bills without a second thought. Our children's lives are precious in ways beyond material value. We felt a sense of moral duty to tackle this and pay the cost because we could afford it, whereas many younger couples would not have the equity in their homes to do so.

We hoped that an investigation into William's death would prevent the deaths of other babies under similar circumstances. The more we learned of obstetrics in private practice, the more we burned for change as a way of justice for William and all the other babies who may have gone through a similar ordeal.

**Day One of the Inquest into William's Death**

The first day of Hearing of Evidence dawned on Tuesday, 5 December in 2006. An inquest is not a criminal trial; it is an investigation by a coroner with a view to establishing cause of death and determining if future improvements can be made for public health and safety. So to us, the obstetrician's choice of lawyer was over the top, akin to using a bulldozer to crack a walnut. He had hired a criminal defence lawyer, when we were simply trying to ascertain why William had died and hopefully prevent the same circumstances that led to his death from happening to future babies.

I was called to take the witness stand and was sworn in, before our barrister commenced questioning me about my evidence. When she had concluded, the obstetrician's criminal defence lawyer stood up. A ruddy-faced man with a shiny nose, wearing a suit, he looked for all the world like a B-grade real-estate salesman. Until I glanced into his eyes. This man was not my friend. I let my gaze slide away from him and looked at the coroner. His questions would be asked on behalf of the court, but only my answers would form the evidence, not his questions. I thought of William and focused. I needed to speak for him, to the coroner. This was my chance.

"Mrs Keays, I take it you're not medically qualified?"

"No," I replied, stating the bleeding obvious.

This was his segue into letting the court know that he would not be asking me about my concerns about medical practices as I was not medically qualified and that he would put those types of questions to the expert medical witnesses.

In a condescending tone, he began to drone on about the amount of correspondence I'd sent to the coroner. I felt like he made vague, and at times derogatory, references to the overall content. He ended the meaningless waffle with words like, "Haven't you?" or "Do you understand?"

Inwardly, my resentment flared at the precious time being wasted by this lawyer playing what felt to me like silly, patriarchal games. I was there for the truth about William's death, not to provide his overweening ego with a stage. I doubled down and readied myself for the next question, reminding myself I was there to be William's voice.

His next verbal volley proceeded to paint me as a medically unqualified woman falsely accusing his eminently respectable client of conspiring to hide or conceal things from the court. He then went on to ask if I was serious. My reply was that I had asked questions to which I still did not know the answers.

Becoming ever more disdainful, he went on to ask if I still persisted in asking the coroner to investigate if there was a cover-up, a conspiracy? He was trying to make me look stupid.

I replied mildly that there were anomalies in the records and that some of the records had been altered after the fact, and that this raised questions for me.

Like a shark moving in for the kill, he demanded that I show them where the records were altered. He said I was suggesting, stating, that the 'professionals' in the hospital had altered the records. Again, he demanded I show them where. There was not one single 'please' amongst all these demands, but I would not allow his calculated rudeness and disrespect to distract me from the truth.

I replied that I had the CTG trace and the medical records sent to me by the hospital, and that they differed from the CTG presented as evidence to the court. The original CTG trace given to the court had several notations on it that the photocopy sent to me did not! These notations could only have been made *after* the photocopied records that I received weeks after William's death.

Let's take a moment to digest this crucial fact. The CTG trace is the physical printout of William's heart rate. It also recorded the contractions of my womb and, therefore, was perhaps the most important piece of evidence in the inquest. The foetal heartrate is a direct reflection of the level of oxygenation to a baby's brain, according to one of the expert witnesses who would provide their opinions later in the inquest.

These pieces of paper were the physical trace, the picture, the *evidence* of William's fight for life and decline into death by protracted starvation of oxygen to his brain, second by second, heartbeat by heartbeat. I received my copies of the medical records *more than two months* after William's death. The additional notations on the CTG presented to the coroner were *not on mine!*

To my mind, I had just proved that at least one part of the medical records had been deliberately altered well after William's death. I hoped fervently that the reporters were writing this down. Not only was it altered retrospectively, both Jim and I maintained that the trace from 3:00 pm to 3:45 pm was missing – a crucial part of the trace. Under cross examination, the midwife would admit to altering the CTG trace in several places after William's death. Our barrister would later show that there were other notations, which both the midwife and obstetrician denied making.

It felt like being trapped in a nightmare, or a horror movie, where you keep screaming out the truth of what happened, and everyone acts as though you hadn't even spoken. I was seeking the truth as a means of change for the greater good, but it felt to me like the other side was attempting to shut me down and discredit me at every turn. In football terms, I was playing the ball, but they were playing the man.

For the rest of the day, the obstetrician's lawyer interrogated me on the witness stand to the point where the coroner felt compelled to interrupt and explain to me why she was allowing it to continue. One of his favourite words for any of my questions or concerns that was not on the medical records or different from what was on the retrospectively altered records was 'speculation'. More than once, I heard something along the lines of, "You're just speculating, aren't you, Mrs Keays?"

He would slowly spell out words to me like I was a child, and end his sentences with words like, "It's confusing, isn't it?"

I suppose it's all part of the theatre of court, but really, what he was deflecting attention away from is that the time for any *theatre*, in our opinion, had been before 4:30 pm on Saturday, 1 November, 2003, instead of 75 minutes later.

Our quietly relentless, brilliant barrister would later unpick much of this on the witness stand. Under her cross examination, the obstetrician and midwife would admit to retrospectively writing their notes. The midwife would also admit to making alterations to the original printout of the CTG trace (both of which formed part of the records used as evidence for the inquest) in full knowledge that William had died.

Surely now, with such evidence, the police would have to investigate.

Our son had died and both Jim and I knew that the times being presented as evidence on the medical records were very different from our own experience on the day.

**Day Two: Wednesday, 6 December 2006**

The obstetrician was in the witness stand. We sat listening to this man as he swore that he had explained to us the risks associated with induction and that I had still agreed to be induced. Both Jim and I were gutted when we realised we'd been had. We trusted this specialist with our son's life. He'd convinced us that leaving William to grow inside my womb could harm him, and now he was denying that he had said that. The betrayal of trust left us feeling sick at heart.

We watched and listened as the obstetrician's criminal defence lawyer talked him through my history of pregnancy and childbirth before commencing on the medical records for my pregnancy with William. I ignored any humiliation I felt while they publicly discussed my very personal information. I'd known this would happen. This was not about me, it was about William and the welfare of future babies. As the day progressed, the testimony moved on to the day of William's birth and death. The obstetrician's retrospectively-written records were verbally elaborated upon, almost three years after the fact. Like mine, the obstetrician's spoken words would form part of the evidence presented to court.

The records were broken down and examined in detail, with the obstetrician being given the opportunity to paint a picture that his brief, retrospectively scrawled medical notes from 2003 did not. I watched and cried as the CTG trace, the one that commenced at 3:45 pm and also had retrospectively written notations on it, was put up on a projector and examined in minute detail. These two middle aged men continued to paint a picture with their words, verbally picking apart the CTG trace and interpreting it in ways that downplayed or cast doubt on the veracity of every anomaly and indicator of foetal distress. Until it came to the part, after the obstetrician turned on the syntocinon for the second time, when they could no longer deny that William was in serious trouble. To look at that trace is to watch my son's death throes. William's heartrate plunged to the bottom of the graph, struggled back up, then plunged again repeatedly as he fought for his life.

The records state that William was born at 5:53 pm. That's almost three hours after we know he first showed an irregular heart rate.

**Day Three: Friday, 8 December 2006**

Two days on, the inquest continued with further cross examination of the obstetrician. This concluded in the afternoon, after which the midwife was sworn in.

To Jim and myself, one crucial part of the midwife's statement was the fact that she had been rostered to finish at 3:00 pm on the day of William's birth.

Crucially, 3:00 pm is the pivot point around which everything centres. It is when I first told the midwife that my contractions had commenced.

We did not know at the time that the midwife was due to clock off at 3:00 pm.

We know she connected me to the CTG at 3:00 pm, yet there is no CTG trace in the records between 3:00 pm and 3:45 pm. This missing 45 minutes of CTG trace is why I asked repeatedly for police investigation over the course of the inquest and afterwards.

It was stated that the midwife commenced the syntocinon drip at 2:20 pm. The midwife was not with me the whole time after the commencement of synthetic oxytocin, nor was she with me the whole time after I advised her that I was in labour. We know it was Jim who first saw William's heartrate dipping on the digital readout and alerted the midwife, who was in another room.

Under cross examination, the midwife admitted that she made notations on the CTG trace four days after William's birth, whilst reviewing it at a meeting. The problem here, to my way of thinking, is that they were reviewing it in full knowledge that William had died and that the coroner had taken William's body for investigation.

There was more writing – though not on the photocopies sent to me – which the midwife denied writing. If that is true, then it appears that William's medical records were a free for all, with any interested party having carte blanche to alter them as they saw fit. It follows that if the midwife or obstetrician did not write those particular notations on the medical records presented to the coroner as evidence, then they had to have been written by someone who was not even there at the time… after William died.

The midwife's evidence continued to be inconsistent when questioned about the second dose of syntocinon. At first, she stated it was only on for 1–2 minutes, then later said it was for a couple of contractions.

Before long, the day came to a close and court adjourned until March 2007, not a moment too soon for the midwife and obstetrician. Our barrister was doing exactly what I had asked of her – shining a light on the darkness. She was shredding the midwife's story.

In publicly questioning the safety of induction by synthetic oxytocin in private hospitals, I was exposing the underbelly of obstetrics in private practice to the light of public scrutiny. I was also striking at the black heart of unnecessary medical intervention for profit.

In my letter to the coroner in December 2004, an excerpt of which is in Chapter Eleven, I raised some serious and horrifying questions about the length of time taken for William to be born after the obstetrician came in and switched on the drug. When questioned on the witness stand, the obstetrician derided any suggestion that things had been slowed down, describing it as absurd.

Yet, it seems someone must have been there, watching and listening as the doctors and their medico-legal lawyers did their utmost to crucify me as an 'absurd' conspiracy theorist. Someone who knew the anaesthetist who was one of the key players in the operating theatre that day, or perhaps the anaesthetist himself, had been watching from the public gallery. How else to explain that same anaesthetist voluntarily stepping forward to provide the police attached to the coroner's office with a statement detailing his concerns about delays in commencing surgery and aspects of William's resuscitation?

The front page headline of the *Sunday Age* newspaper:

**"Baby-death doctor speaks out"**

**Carmel Egan**
March 4, 2007 – 11.00 am

*AN ANAESTHETIST plagued by his conscience and sleepless nights has defied the medical profession's code of silence to speak out about the death of a newborn baby at [the private hospital].*

*[The anaesthetist's] 11th-hour decision to provide new evidence to the coroners court has brought to a halt an inquest on the death of William Grant Keays.*

*William was stillborn on November 1, 2003, but revived to live for 6½ hours.*

*Now the on-call anaesthetist who attended his birth has claimed there were unexplained delays and a questionable standard of care in the baby's emergency caesarean delivery and resuscitation. [The anaesthetist] has raised concerns about the time taken to get William's mother to surgery after the baby became distressed during a prolonged, medically induced labour.*

*In an email to the court, [the anaesthetist] said there were further delays before the emergency caesarean was performed, delays in inserting a tube into William's windpipe, its placement in his oesophagus instead of his trachea, and delays in beginning external cardiac compressions.*

*His death is being investigated by the coroner at the request of his parents, Karin and Jim Keays. Mr Keays is well-known as a singer with the group Cotton, Keays, Morris and as former singer for 1960s rock group Masters Apprentices.*

*The inquest into their son's death has been adjourned while further information is sought from [the anaesthetist] and other potential witnesses.*

*William was four days overdue when Mrs Keays was booked into [the private hospital] by her obstetrician (name withheld).*

*She was given intravenous syntocinon, a drug used to induce contractions, under the supervision of associate midwife (name withheld).*

*Hours later the baby's heart rate plummeted and an emergency caesarean was performed but it was too late to save William's life.*

*"Some days following this incident I contacted by phone the then chief executive officer of [the private hospital] and relayed my concerns to him about aspects of the baby's resuscitation," [the anaesthetist] said.*

*"I wished, with his help, to arrange a meeting between myself and [the paediatricians] where these matters could be discussed. This meeting did not eventuate."*

*[The anaesthetist] then wrote to the Medical Defence Association to outline his concerns.*

*Mrs Keays yesterday said her aim was to avoid a repeat of what happened to her child and added: "I am very grateful to [the anaesthetist], who has our full support."*

*She said: "Our heartfelt wish is that [the anaesthetist] does not hold back one single thing."*

*The inquest has been adjourned to June.*

Jim and I had no previous inkling that there were any issues with William's resuscitation. The paediatrician had been handed a baby with no signs of life. It was an emergency situation. I've never forgotten the urgency in the anaesthetist's voice in theatre on that day when he said he was going over to help resuscitate William. Neither Jim nor I are vindictive or unreasonable people. We understood that people make errors at work, especially under pressure in an emergency, but the obstetrician and the midwife did not appear to us to be under pressure when commencing the artificial induction of my labour and, it seemed to us, they actually created an emergency between them by doing so. By this, I mean that an emergency was created by inducing William, leading to foetal distress. Jim and I felt they then failed to rectify that emergency situation in time to prevent the harm caused to William. Unbelievably, to us at any rate, the obstetrician later testified that there was nothing to indicate it was an emergency, even after the midwife had turned off the syntocinon and contacted the obstetrician about William's abnormal CTG trace. Even after he arrived and noted late decelerations in William's heart rate he still reintroduced the syntocinon. Even after observing the subsequent effects on the CTG trace, he still would not call it an emergency, saying that he called the anaesthetist at that point because the trace was severely abnormal and the baby needed immediate delivery as quickly as they could deliver it.

While our focus remained on the actions and inactions of the obstetrician and midwife, and what part that played in William being suffocated to death over a long period of time, we welcomed the information in the statement from the anaesthetist. Breaking the medical code of silence can't have been an easy thing for him to do and we were immensely grateful for his integrity in doing so. We particularly looked forward to the coroner investigating the anaesthetist's statement.

One week later, the *Sunday Age* headlines blazed:

**Revealed: second mum tells of hospital baby tragedy**
**"How many deaths have occurred?"**

**Carmel Egan**
March 11, 2007 – 11.00 am

*A BABY died during labour at Melbourne's [the private hospital] just two months after baby William Keays whose controversial death is being investigated by the coroner, The Sunday Age can reveal.*

*Karyn Kennedy has revealed that her first baby was 10 days overdue when she was admitted to the hospital at 10pm on January 3, 2004.*

*The daughter she named Saoirse (pronounced Seer-sha) was delivered stillborn after an emergency caesarean 10 hours later.*

*Karyn and husband Andrew have decided to speak out in support of anaesthetist [the anaesthetist], who attended both Mrs Kennedy and William Keays' mother, Karin.*

*The Sunday Age last week reported [the anaesthetist's] 11th-hour bid to reveal previously undisclosed details about William's resuscitation and concerns about delays in his delivery.*

*[The anaesthetist's] action brought the long-running Keays' inquest to a dramatic adjournment last week.*

*In an email to the court [the anaesthetist] also said his requests for follow-up meetings with the then chief executive officer of [the private hospital] and others present at William's birth were ignored.*

*"It just makes me wonder if our situation would be different if those meetings did take place," Ms Kennedy said.*

*"There is no way of telling, but it concerns me that these issues have been brought up not just by a mother whose baby died but by a member of the staff.*

*"How many deaths have occurred since, and would we be leading a different life now if those meetings did take place?*

*"It is something that horrifies Andrew and me."*

The Kennedys also want to support Jim and Karin Keays in their quest to find out why their healthy, full-term baby died.

William was stillborn at [the private hospital] but was revived. He died in his parents' arms 6½ hours later on November 1, 2003.

Because William drew breath, his death is registered and able to be investigated by the coroner.

Saoirse could not be revived and there will be no public examination of her death.

*"In William's case his was a neonatal classification, which won him the right to a hearing in the coroners court, but stillbirths slip under the radar,"* Mr Kennedy said.

The Kennedys are distressed there is no public investigation of unexplained stillbirths.

Although the Consultative Council on Obstetric and Pediatric Mortality and Morbidity is responsible for examining and recording stillbirths, details of individual cases remain confidential.

Details are not revealed to the parents.

*"Babies are dying and it gets no exposure or follow-up,"* Mrs Kennedy said.

*"Every government department that we have approached in this situation has slammed their door in our faces.*

*"We believe there is enough to be concerned about in our case that warrants an investigation.*

*"As well as putting our own minds to rest, we want to make sure it never happens again.*

*"What they are doing to the parents... it's cruel."*

Karyn and Andrew do not normally use the term stillborn when speaking of Saoirse; they prefer to say she was born sleeping.

Pictures of them cradling their dark-haired, olive-skinned baby are proudly on display in their home.

Two years ago the Kennedys had another baby girl, named Asha (meaning one who brings hope), and they are expecting their third child to be born within days.

It seemed, at last, that things were shifting towards the truth and maybe even justice. The following week, for the third Sunday in a row, the front page of the *Sunday Age* declared:

**"Coroner acts on stillbirth law"**

*VICTORIA'S coroner will challenge the law by investigating the stillbirth of a baby girl, following revelations in The Sunday Age about her death in a private Melbourne hospital.*

*In an unprecedented move, the coroner has informed Saoirse Kennedy's parents that medical records of her delivery on January 4, 2004, at [the private hospital] are being reviewed and may be referred to an inquest.*

*Such an inquest would be a first in Australia and a challenge to coronial laws across all states and territories. The move will shock*

Victoria's medico-legal community because stillbirths are outside the jurisdiction of the coroners court.

It is also an unprecedented challenge by the court for the State Government to overhaul existing laws.

But for Saoirse's parents, Karyn and Andrew Kennedy, it is overdue recognition.

"This validates Saoirse's life in the eyes of the Victorian law and means the world to us," Mrs Kennedy said.

"She was real, she did exist, she was important. And even though she was only here for a short period of time, her life has achieved great things," she said. "All any parent could ever hope is that their child's life amounts to something. We are no different.

"Our motives in pursuing an investigation remain pure. We seek the truth about why our daughter died, and ultimately assist in achieving changes to reduce the number of deaths each year."

Coroner's court chief executive Michele Gardner would not discuss the ramifications of her decision but confirmed Saoirse's case was being reviewed. "After representations from the family and a meeting with the family, the coroner has agreed to review medical records to ascertain matters of fact," Ms Gardner said.

Attorney-General Rob Hulls declined to comment.

But in a letter to the Kennedys dated March 13 and signed by him, he wrote: "Thank you for your letter of 6 October, 2006, concerning the appropriate jurisdiction for the investigation of stillbirths.

*"You have taken time to make a thoughtful contribution to the review by the Victorian Parliament Law Reform Committee of the Coroner's Act 1985 with the purpose of improving Victoria's approach to perinatal deaths.*

*"Since the committee made its recommendations, considerable policy analysis and consultation has been undertaken. The government (response)... is being prepared."*

*For 10 years there has been no change in the rate of healthy, full-term babies dying in labour or delivery in Victorian hospitals.*

*There are an average 600 stillbirths of foetuses over 20 weeks gestation in Victoria each year, of which about 16 per cent are unexplained.*

*In its 2004 report the Consultative Council of Obstetric and Paediatric Mortality and Morbidity recorded 10 stillbirths and 13 neonatal deaths from peripartum hypoxia (lack of oxygen) and identified several cases where deficiencies were identified in intrapartum management or neonatal resuscitation.*

*"Such cases always warrant careful review at the institution where the birth occurred," the report noted.*

*The Kennedys spoke out last week because their repeated appeals for answers from legal, medical and bureaucratic authorities had been rejected or ignored for three years.*

*Their first letter to the coroner was sent in early 2004, they made a submission to the law reform review committee, they wrote repeatedly to the Health Services Commissioner, they wrote to Mr Hulls in October 2006 and again to the coroner last month pointing out similarities between their case and that of baby William Keays.*

*As revealed in The Sunday Age last week, Saoirse Kennedy was stillborn at [the private hospital] just eight weeks after William Keays died there on November 1, 2003.*

*William was delivered stillborn but was revived to survive for several hours. Saoirse could not be revived.*

*In legal terms, one breath separates their tragedies. Because William drew a breath he is the subject of an inquest. Until this week the Kennedys had no such recourse.*

*Bereavement and the pursuit of answers has drawn the two families together.*

*"Parents and families expect that such dangerous anomalies within in the law would be promptly changed once they are identified," said William's mother, Karin Keays.*

*"We are so very happy for Saoirse's family and wish them well for the coronial investigation. This is a courageous decision and a victory for commonsense," she said.*

*Chair of the consultative council Professor James King gave his support to the coroner.*

*"The Kennedys and the Keays illustrate precisely the anomaly that exists," Professor King said.*

*"The anomaly (is) where the coroner has full power to investigate when an infant is born and takes a breath and dies, but no power when the baby doesn't take a breath.*

"The council is seeking the power to refer exceptional, unexplained stillbirths to the coroner.

"The coroner does not want to have anything to do with that (late-term terminations) but we don't propose that. We didn't recommend that the coroner should have some kind of mandatory requirement to investigate all stillbirths."

[The private hospital], which has about 900 births a year, defended its reputation for maternity services.

Chief executive officer Graham Clarke said his hospital had delivered babies for 35 years and employed an experienced team of midwives.

"[The Keays and Kennedy cases] are very rare circumstances that unfortunately occurred within a short period of time of each other, and are extremely tragic for both the parents and staff of the hospital," Mr Clarke said.

"We will continue to fully co-operate with the coroner's inquest investigating the incidents surrounding the neonatal death of baby William Keays in 2003."

The bombshell evidence from the anaesthetist and the publicity surrounding it meant that proceedings were further adjourned until 22 May 2007.

I'd never heard the term 'expert witness' prior to the inquest. Expert witness doctors can charge thousands of dollars to provide a written opinion or to appear in court to testify, even though the legal process requires their expert opinions for the judge or coroner to make an informed decision. An expert witness asked to give evidence for another doctor may have their fees covered by the doctor's medical indemnity insurance. Families of the deceased pay the bills for expert witnesses themselves, if they can find an expert witness to support their case at all.

Our barrister had only been able to find one expert witness who would in any way criticise William's medical treatment. We dutifully agreed to pay the four-figure fees for his services. When I finally read through his expert witness statement, my heart sank. His criticism was based on what appeared to me to be a misunderstanding of the evidence. I made notes of the anomalies in the report and sent them to our barrister.

Our barrister then sent the report back to the expert witness for revision. The result was that he had no criticism to make of the obstetrician.

It was now clear to me that accepted standard practices in Australian obstetrics were far below what was acceptable to me, and to any parent. I wanted to know if it was the same in other developed countries and asked our barrister if we could obtain an opinion from an expert witness in the UK.

The obstetrician and at least one of his expert witnesses were members of RCOG (the Royal College of Obstetricians and Gynaecologists), the British version of RANZCOG. During his testimony, the obstetrician had proudly boasted that he had been 'elevated' to being a member of the British college so I wanted to know what that college would have to say about his conduct at and around the time of William's birth. Our barrister warned me that it was unlikely that the court would accept the opinion of an expert witness from overseas. Undeterred, I asked her to see if one could be procured from a fellow of RCOG.

My own research had led me to a referral for one Marsden Wagner, a perinatologist and perinatal epidemiologist from California who served as Director of Maternal and Child Health for the California State Health Department, Director of the University of Copenhagen-UCLA Health Research Center, and Director of Women's and Children's Health for the World Health Organization. So eminently qualified was this man, I could hardly believe it when I received his reply, feeling fortunate that he even spared the time to read through my letters and email. His response pulled no punches in his assessment of the state obstetrics in Australia and his own experience of dealing with the obstetric profession here.

Although it was what we already knew, it was still shocking to read in black and white the confirmation of what we were up against.

Meanwhile, as I had requested, our barrister had gone ahead with procuring a professional opinion from an expert witness in Great Britain. Mr John Pogmore was a Fellow of the Royal College of Obstetrics and Gynaecology (RCOG) in the UK and an examiner for the Membership examination of that college – the same college to which the Australian obstetrician and expert witness were so proud to belong. This, though, did not stop the lawyers from objecting to Mr Pogmore's expert opinion being heard by the coroner at William's inquest.

Mr Pogmore had also been a consultant obstetrician and gynaecologist since July 1978 and latterly at the Birmingham Women's Hospital until June, 2004. In addition, he had been Honorary Senior Clinical Lecturer in Obstetrics and Gynaecology to the Birmingham University Medical School until June, 2004. Mr Pogmore's introduction specifically noted that "I am used to dealing with patients who have inductions of labour, large babies and are post mature by dates."

Like Marsden Wagner in the USA, Mr Pogmore was eminently qualified to examine and to give his expert opinion on every aspect of William's medical treatment and care. Like Marsden Wagner, his assessment of the actions and events around William's birth was very different from the opinions of his Australian counterparts.

The medical defence teams jumped straight up and made their displeasure regarding the media publicity very clear to the coroner. The criminal defence lawyer proceeded to publicly censure Jim and me for providing a photo of William to the newspaper, referring to William as "the baby". This was deeply distressing for Jim and me as we were, and always will be, proud of our big, strong baby boy. In appearance, he was a masculine version of Holly and Bonnie. Three peas from the same pod. We sat, sickened and enraged, as the legal equivalent of a hyena attempted to dehumanise William by not using his name and spoke of his baby photos as though they were shameful and not fit to be seen.

No doubt there had been much lobbying and pressure from certain quarters because we were told there was to be no further investigation of the anaesthetist's statement, and there would be no inquest or coronial investigation for Saoirse Kennedy. Any talk of the coroner challenging the law was effectively hosed down.

The midwife resumed the witness stand and thereafter it was like watching a superhero action movie where the previously mild-mannered incognito hero sheds their disguise and takes control over the villains. In a macabre yet graceful dance, our barrister pivoted and lunged, withdrew and circled before closing her well-laid traps on the hapless midwife time and again. The truth was her sword and she used it to cut through the carefully constructed defence over and over.

Under questioning by our barrister, the midwife testified that, sometime soon after William's death, she was asked to write down her recollection of events as they occurred. Had our barrister not pursued it, we would never have known of the existence of the document. When asked to produce it, she said she didn't have it, that it was probably given to the head of midwifery. Our mildly spoken barrister was relentless, eliciting the previously unknown information, to us anyway, that she had a copy at home. Handwritten clearly across the top of the page of this previously secret document was, 'CONFIDENTIAL. PREPARED IN ANTICIPATION OF LITIGATION', but the midwife said she didn't remember writing that. Later, she said that she probably did write it... that someone else probably instructed her to write that.

Hearing this felt like a knife through my heart; knowing how, at the time that document was being written, I'd been trying so hard to project forgiveness and compassion to everyone involved with William's death. To hear the hard evidence of the calculated damage control that took place in anticipation of a law suit... within days of William's death... the betrayal of trust was a blow to my guts that took my breath away. We weren't even thinking of contacting the coroner just after William's death, but they were preparing for the lawsuit they knew was coming from us. My thoughts went briefly to the first time Jim and I saw the midwife after William's death as we sat outside the private hospital. No wonder she'd looked so alarmed and had so little to say.

Our barrister went on to explore at length how it was that the second dose of synthetic oxytocin was not written in hospital records *nor* in her statement. To my way of thinking, it effectively made the midwife's statement incorrect. She replied that she didn't know "we" did it that way. Our superhero barrister was not letting her get away with anything, forcing her to admit the statement was made with the hospital's solicitor, that it was actually the solicitor who wrote the statement for her and she signed it. It wasn't the only time she spoke with hospital solicitors about the events around William's birth and death, either. Once again, our barrister elicited from the midwife that she had "a number" of conferences with solicitors.

During a break in court, I was on my way to the bathroom, my mind mulling over what I had heard. It felt like my nurse friend's prediction was coming true. She had warned that they would try to sweep the whole thing under the carpet.

She had said that, if pushed, they would try to put the blame on me, and try they did. It happened in subtle but very deliberate ways, like the language used in the obstetrician's testimony that put the onus on me for things that no woman can control.

It happened every time he said things during his testimony like, "SHE had a contraction here" and "SHE had a deceleration here" and "SHE was only 4 cm dilated" and (in his unsubstantiated opinion only) cause of death was "an unexplained placental malfunction".

It felt like he was using language designed to deflect responsibility onto me, the mother, as though I had any control over my contractions. A woman cannot control a contraction, but doctors can and *do* when they give her drugs to induce, speed up and slow down labour.

A deceleration is a deceleration of *William's* heart rate, yet throughout his testimony, the obstetrician said "SHE" has a deceleration here.

It looked to me like the last part of my nurse friend's prediction was coming true and that, if they couldn't blame me, the blame would be shifted onto the nursing staff. The midwife was taking the fall for it, just as my friend had predicted.

Suddenly, as I was walking through the foyer, the midwife appeared before me, flanked by two people who looked like legal types, professionally dressed. They stood there blocking my path so that I would have had to deviate to walk around them. The midwife was looking at me intently, a little old woman, her eyes brimming with tears. Situational memory and PTSD kicked in and I was instantly transported back to the operating theatre with this woman's tear-filled eyes looking down on me. The whole thing would have taken less than ten seconds. I spoke a few words of forgiveness to her and she said she felt so sorry for me. Naively, I thought she was apologising for what happened to William.

Then I stepped past them and continued on. When I returned to court, I told our barrister that I'd seen the midwife. She looked at me sharply and asked if I'd spoken to her. I said yes and knew immediately that something was very wrong.

Court resumed and the hospital's lawyers approached the coroner saying that Mrs Keays had spoken with the midwife and did not blame her for what happened. There was some dialogue between the lawyers and the coroner, then the midwife was excused from having to give any further evidence. It was all over and done with very quickly. The now-retired midwife was free to leave for her planned trip overseas and I was left wondering what had happened.

Our barrister, to her credit, did not berate me for speaking with a sworn witness. It's probably one of the oldest, dirtiest tricks in the book, and I'd fallen for it. Although the midwife was out of the witness box during the break, she was still sworn in. By speaking to her when she and her party stepped into my path, I had unwittingly given them an out. To me, it showed how desperate they were because our barrister had been tearing holes in her story, exposing the untruths and inconsistencies one after the other. In the end, even that small justice for William was not served.

**Day Five: Monday, 4 June 2007**

Another expert witness was sworn in: yet another middle-aged man full of self-importance as he confirmed his credentials. Like the obstetrician, he was proud to be a fellow of the British College, RCOG. This doctor was also a member of the CCOPMM, which stands for Consultative Council on Obstetric and Paediatric Mortality and Morbidity. It is one of the in-house medical committees which most people have no idea exist.

William's death was reviewed by this group, as was Saoirse's, but neither family nor the public are ever allowed to know the details or outcome of their reviews despite our requests. It's all kept in-house between the doctors. Once again, I wondered, were the members of this group paid with public monies? Because if they were, there should be transparency and readily available access to their information by the public.

Whilst this doctor would not criticise his fellow obstetrician for turning on the syntocinon for the second time, he admitted that he probably would not have done it himself.

Our barrister then began her cross examination, questioning the appropriateness of this man giving independent evidence. Not only was he a long-term colleague of the obstetrician in question, he was a business partner of the sonographer who examined me during my pregnancy. He himself had also seen me twice as a patient in previous years. This seemed to me to be way too many conflicts of interest for him to be considered impartial. I wondered why his opinion as an expert witness was accepted at all.

The expert witness stated more than once that I agreed to induction because I was uncomfortable and that it suited me. More silent screaming from me. How could such an important investigation into a death be based on an assumption by someone who wasn't even there? Jim and I had been adamant and very vocal from the start that this was definitely *not* the reason why we had agreed to induction.

Our barrister stopped him and confirmed that his understanding of the situation was that there was no medical reason for the induction of labour and it was done for the convenience of those involved. She then put it to him that, given our reluctance to be induced, if the obstetrician was truly concerned about William's size then it would have been good practice to have suggested to me that an ultrasound be done. The expert agreed. Despite this, he arrogantly refused to agree that women should be advised of the possible risks associated with the use of syntocinon.

Marsden Wagner's warning to me about the Australian obstetrics profession sprang to mind.

I learned a lot in the course of the inquest. I learned that, in 2001, the *Australian and New Zealand Journal of Obstetrics* published an article by Dr Spencer and Dr McLennan declaring that emergency caesarean times in Australia were taking a lot longer than recommended. The article went on to say that the UK and USA obstetric colleges have recommended that the 'decision-to-incision' time for emergency caesareans should be a maximum of 30 minutes. The RANZCOG guidelines in 2003 also stated 30 minutes decision-to-incision time as optimal.

In their article, Dr Spencer and Dr McLennan worked out their findings based on three levels of hospital:

**Level 3** is a large public hospital with resident staff, paediatric and anaesthetic staff, close on-call access to a senior obstetrician and a dedicated obstetric theatre.

**Level 2** hospitals had some resident staff, paediatric and anaesthetic staff but not 24-hour access to theatres.

**Level 1** private hospitals, like the one where I gave birth to Bonnie and William, had no resident staff. Care in labour was given by midwives working shifts and visiting medical staff.

The study showed that the average time from decision to incision in Level 1 hospitals in Australia was **one hour and nine minutes** – more than double the 30 minutes expected by the Royal

College in the UK and the American College for an urgent caesarean section.

I learned all this retrospectively and at the cost of William's life. With this knowledge, I would never have agreed to be induced at a Level 1 private hospital. Every minute of an abnormal heartrate is another minute of reduced oxygen to a baby's brain, and the possibility of brain injury as a result.

**Day Six: Tuesday, 5 June 2007**

There were now several written submissions of Australian expert witness opinions before the court. Predictably, some were long winded pontifications, sometimes differing wildly when it came to conjecturing about what mysterious, unsubstantiated physical ailment may have been responsible for William's death.

Meanwhile, our barrister had asked the British expert witness, Mr Pogmore, to comment on the reintroduction of syntocinon by the obstetrician when he arrived after being called in by the midwife about my 'concerning' CTG trace.

It seemed odd to me that his previous opinion had not addressed this because it was such a critical point in William's tiny life. In a different time zone, on the other side of the world, this experienced Fellow of the Royal College of Obstetricians and Gynaecologists examined the documents and responded swiftly and emphatically.

Mr Pogmore's response began with him clearly stating that he did not appear to have been given the same notes (previously).

Now I knew why he had not previously commented on the reintroduction of syntocinon. He hadn't known about it. Once again, Mr Pogmore's assessment and expert opinion was almost opposite to every single one of the Australian experts.

His expert opinion confirmed what we had already worked out for ourselves.

The opinion of every single Australian expert witness contradicted the opinion of Mr Pogmore, and Marsden Wagner's informal assessment, on crucial points. It was extremely disturbing and it was what we hoped to change.

**Day Seven: Wednesday, 6 June 2007**

The final day of hearing of evidence arrived. Despite the obstetrician responsible for William's health and safety proudly declaring himself to have been 'elevated' as a member of the British RCOG, and at least one other expert witness also being a member of the UK College, Mr Pogmore's expert opinion was not heard. Although our legal team had Mr Pogmore on standby in the UK, regardless of the time difference, ready and willing to testify remotely via video, this was disallowed. Our barrister had warned us that this might happen. Marsden Wagner had told us straight up. More silent screaming from me at the injustice of it all. Now, I just wanted the whole thing to be done with.

The day proceeded with Australian expert witnesses including the retired obstetrician we had procured and to whom I'd sent back his original opinion for revision because it was so flawed. This obstetrician had been booked to appear as the final expert witness via video in court at our expense, of course. I had become numbed to the wholesale gouging of our mortgage by these people. As I sat there and watched him torpedo our case, putting the final boot into William, I did myself a favour and tuned out, turning my attention to making notes in preparation for my statement to the coroner on behalf of the family.

The written opinions of the Australian expert witnesses, along with their oral evidence in court, were examined at length during the inquest. Their opinions form part of the court transcript of the inquest into William's death and are historically documented, forever available for future reference. Unfortunately, the eminently qualified expert opinion of Mr Pogmore and the words of Marsden Wagner do not form part of the court transcripts.

In the coroner's finding at the conclusion of the inquest, the coroner refers to the first of the two opinions from Mr Pogmore, and the legal rationale for declining to hear viva voce his evidence. For more information, a link to the finding can be found at the back of this book.

*

In the course of the inquest, I recalled there had been a lot of media hype in 2003 about obstetricians threatening to leave in droves because of the crippling cost of medical indemnity insurance. The inference was that obstetricians were being unfairly targeted by women suing them when things went wrong. Like most people, I suppose, I felt sorry for the doctors, as we were meant to.

Ironically, I spoke to our obstetrician about this at one of my antenatal visits with William in my tummy. He told me that obstetrics is a young man's game and that he would be getting out of it in the next couple of years. Alarmed, I asked if he would still be around for William's birth and he said he would. I remember feeling relieved.

I also learned that the Federal Government already subsidised 80% of the cost of medical indemnity insurance for obstetricians. The publicity in 2003 was about putting pressure on the state governments to cover the cost of the remaining 20%! I was at first dumbfounded, then felt silly when I remembered my discussion with the obstetrician. Of course, he hadn't said anything to me about the government paying his insurance with our tax dollars. I was also told at one point that some state governments did indeed cover the remaining 20%, to varying degrees. If this is the case, obstetricians in some states would have 100% of their medical indemnity paid for by public monies. In other states, marginally less. Put simply, we – every Australian taxpayer, irrespective of income – are paying for these lawyers to exonerate doctors from any wrongdoing that causes injury or the death of our loved ones.

With this knowledge, I reflected on the publicity of 2003 and realised it must have been generated by spin doctors for the medical industry. I also realised that the publicity disappeared quickly and I never read or heard anything reported about the outcome, presumably once a deal had been struck. After that, the blinkers fell away regarding any media publicity relating to the medical industry. Now, when I see or hear media reports relating to the medical and pharmaceutical industries, I ask myself, "What is the real agenda here?"

I wrote to the office of the Federal Minister for Health to obtain confirmation of this information, only to be told that I would have to put my questions separately to each state and territory as a formal request under the Freedom of Information Act. Like the church of old, the medical industry has power and influence with carte blanche over our hard-earned tax dollars.

*

If I had my time over again, knowing what I know now, I would trust my body and my own birth history. I would find a registered independent midwife, maybe along with a doula, and give birth at home.

"What if something went wrong?" I hear you ask. Well, it couldn't go any more wrong than it went at the private hospital with a private obstetrician, could it? After listening to all the testimony presented at William's inquest, I have come full circle to the same conclusion that I began with. Without the use of the synthetic oxytocin, I can see no indisputable reason why William's birth would not have been as straightforward as Bonnie's and Holly's.

Had homebirth been unavailable to me, or too expensive, I would go only to a Level 3 public hospital and I would not, under any circumstances, agree to artificial induction of labour. From what I heard at the inquest, if a mother or baby has a diagnosed obstetric or medical condition, then artificial induction of labour by syntocinon would not be indicated.

Logically, it follows that if there is no diagnosed medical condition, then any suggestion or recommendation to the mother to undertake artificial induction of labour, along with all the associated risks involved, would be a matter of personal choice rather than medical necessity.

Finally, the big 'what if' question. The obstetrician said after William died, that my baby would have died anyway if left inside my tummy. What if that were true? This question has been mine to ponder at length for many years and I can say, with all of my heart, that if it were preordained that William had to die that day, then I would rather he have been left to drift gently off to sleep, happy and safe in the loving home of my body instead of being drugged, terrified and suffocated to death inside my womb.

I had the premonition. Maybe it was maternal instinct, maybe it was William's spirit speaking to me, maybe it was something bigger than all of us. Wherever it came from, it was very real and very clear. Had I followed my intuition and William had died, it would have appeared to everyone to have been the wrong decision.

Yes, everyone would have pointed the finger of blame at me afterwards for not following the obstetrician's advice, but the doctors tried to blame me anyway, even when I did. Either way, I would have to live with the knowledge that my decision to either trust or not trust the obstetrician may have led to a different outcome. In this hypothetical scenario there is no winning for the mother, but William would have been spared the appalling suffering and terror.

## Chapter Thirteen

## Think About Tomorrow Today

*"The key to immortality is first living a life worth remembering."*
*~ Bruce Lee*

It was on Friday, 15 August 2008 that Jim, Holly, Bonnie and I sat in the coroner's court for the last time. We took the girls out of school so we could be there as a family, united in our love and support for William, even in death. There is a newspaper photo of the four of us, taken as we walked out to the carpark after the coroner had handed down her finding into the inquest of our son and brother, William Grant Keays. The photo tells a little story of its own when you know what to look for. What you cannot see in the photo, is the personality and behavioural changes in Jim, and the effects on our family, that were the result of the high doses of steroids that he regularly took as part of his medical treatment. It was only just over one year since we'd flown back to Melbourne from the UK in the most dramatic of circumstances, after Jim had fallen ill and been diagnosed with multiple myeloma. Back then, we didn't even know if Jim would still be alive in a year.

Prior to beginning the steroids, Jim and I had been as one in our quest for justice for William and change for the wellbeing of future babies. Jim had been my loving husband and life partner for two decades; my rock, my best friend and greatest support, never flinching from my sadness, always ready with open arms and open heart when I could no longer contain my grief. More often than not, Jim would cry with me as we comforted each other. When he began the pharmaceutical treatment, he changed in many ways. Like turning off a light in the flick of a switch, I lost my loving husband, my best friend, my lover and my champion. His body was there, but that was not my husband inside it. It was incredibly confusing and hurtful, another huge grief that I had no idea how to deal with, especially as I'd had no opportunity to even begin healing my maternal grief.

In the photo, we are walking side by side, rugged up against the bitter cold of August in Melbourne in our winter coats. Holly and Jim are on the left. Holly appears to be smiling at something Jim is explaining to her. In fact, she was amused by the antics of the media photographers in front of us, who were dodging around each other backwards as we walked towards them, each trying to get their shot. It was the first time that the girls had seen a media scrum, albeit a small one. Jim's hair is short and uncharacteristically curly, which is how it grew back after chemotherapy. Beneath the winter woollies, Jim's body is thin, his face drawn.

Jim is holding Bonnie's hand. Her little face is pale and she looks pensively towards me and our clasped hands as I scrabble about in my handbag, on the pretext of looking for the car keys. My face looks tense and on the verge of tears and my head is down, kept that way deliberately in an effort to hide my devastation and bitter disappointment at the coroner's finding. From the very first, I had requested police investigation into the missing 45 minutes of CTG trace and the disputed medical records. A death had occurred, William's death, and those responsible for William's safety had altered the records, written them *after* his death. Had it been a workplace death or a road death, there would have been specialist police investigation and heavy penalties, even jail, for anyone whose actions or decisions contributed to that death. Surely, altering or tampering with evidence was a red flag. I could not understand why the same level of investigation did not apply to the death of my baby son.

The coroner's finding made it clear there would be no criminal investigation into William's death and, anticipating that outcome, our lawyers had already commenced a civil suit before the finding. We began the court-ordered process of mediation, which is required before a civil matter can proceed to court to be heard before a judge. I didn't want money for my son's death, I wanted police investigation and that is what I reminded our lawyers, telling them that I would take it to every judge in every court until there was nowhere left to go. Their response was hard-hitting and unequivocal: there would be no police investigation into William's death. If we were to continue down the legal path to court, the cost to each party would be at least $250,000. If we were to lose, and we were told that we would, then we would bear not only our costs but the costs of the other parties. Could we afford to lose three quarters of a million dollars, they asked? Of course not. We weren't lawyers or doctors, we were in the music industry. Musicians don't have that sort of money lying around, nor do they have their legal costs paid for by the Australian public.

I looked at my sick husband and thought of him. He'd had enough of this, enough of anything that did not support him in his quest to live at any cost. I thought of our daughters. There was no telling how much time they had left with their dad. I thought of William, for whom there would be no justice from the Australian legal system. Beggaring our family would not achieve anything for him.

"You've had your win," I was told, "They've halved the dosage of syntocinon since the inquest."

It felt like an insult that anyone would try to equate the value of a human life with money. Our legal counsel was telling us to take what was being offered as compensation, and get on with our lives. To me the money was irrelevant. It didn't feel like a win to me, but I knew I was beaten in my crusade for social justice. Defeated, I didn't ask who 'they' were. There would be no justice for William, but maybe, just maybe, future lives would be saved as a result.

On 29 December 2008, Jim and I sent a letter to the state coroner, who by then was Judge Coate, raising several key issues which we felt were insufficiently explored, including the lack of police investigation into the fundamental differences in the testimony of the midwife to the reality of our experience at the time. We had no idea why Graeme Johnstone was no longer state coroner but presumed that the changeover contributed to the length of the coronial investigation.

The letter in response from the coroner's office in February, 2009 offered some explanation as to why there was no police investigation. We were told that Victoria Police are not generally trained in medical and health related investigations and, as a consequence, feel ill equipped to question health professionals unless there is a matter of potential criminal conduct. It went on to say that the coroner was aware of her capacity to direct a police investigation, if she felt it would assist her in her duties.

That left one last door on which to knock, and that was the Chief Commissioner of Police himself. On 28 April 2009, I sent him a letter detailing the reasons for our request for a police investigation. The summary paragraph of my letter to him included the following:

"On page 1, the value of police investigation into William's death is commented upon. It is my understanding that the Police Coroner's Assistants Unit are assisted by medico-legal personnel and on that basis are very well equipped to investigate medical deaths. Further, **the key to any investigation into William's death lies in the conflicting accounts of the actions and time**

**frame in the hours before his birth and does not necessarily require specialist medical knowledge. It does require an investigation committed to uncovering the truth..."**

In July, I received a letter from the Chief of Staff to the Chief Commissioner, who had obtained material from the coroner's office in order to consider my concerns. He noted that the coroner detected no evidence of criminal conduct to justify investigation by Victoria Police and considered it unlikely that a police investigation would bring to light any new evidence of criminal conduct.

If my son had died in a vehicle accident or in the workplace, there would have been a police investigation to establish if the driver's or employer's actions or decisions had caused his death. From my observations throughout the coronial investigation into William's death, the same standard of investigation does not apply to doctors, nurses and hospitals.

From my perspective, I could only see one conclusion to be reached from both responses: that medical records can be retrospectively altered, disposed of, rewritten or not written at all and it is not considered criminal conduct in the eyes of the law. I felt the coroner had done the best she could with what she had.

I never again referred to the coroner's finding until the time came to write this book fourteen years later. Unable to find a copy of it at home, I wrote to the coroner's office and promptly received one in response. After sharing it with Holly and Bonnie, I was taken aback by their surprised reactions. They were children at the time and had seen only the disillusion and disappointment felt by their parents. Where I had seen only failure on my own part to make any real difference, they saw positive changes as a result of the inquest.

Looking at the finding with the benefit of time and distance, I could see parts where the coroner is critical, or at least doubtful, about some aspects of the case but was unable to reach a definitive conclusion either way.

I read with fresh eyes the coroner's words regarding that pivotal moment when the obstetrician walked in and turned on the synthetic oxytocin drip, going *against* the drug manufacturer's guidelines (unbeknownst to me at the time). The coroner accepted that it was not appropriate in the circumstances to adopt this approach. Still, she was unable to reach a conclusion that it contributed to the outcome (which was William's death by starvation of oxygen).

There were four recommendations by the coroner in the finding as a result of the inquest into William's death:

1. That the RANZCOG prepare an information booklet/sheet about the induction of labour including the indications for, the methods adopted and in what circumstances and recommend to its members the dissemination of this information through their own practices.

2. That the RANZCOG, in consultation with the Department of Human Services and the Australian Private Hospitals Association, prepare a booklet of information addressing issues women should consider in choosing the type of hospital in which to give birth.

3. That the RANZCOG play an educative role to its members by recommending dissemination of information about the differences in services between the public and private maternity facilities be adopted as standard practice by individual obstetricians with private practices.

4. That the RANZCOG take a more proactive role in educating and encouraging its members to adopt a universal best practice of continuous CTG monitoring with syntocinon-induced labour.

Being a public inquest, I had long assumed that the details of the finding would be publicly available to anyone to learn from, but that was not the case. I do not know the reason why. In 2022, I sent a formal request to the coroner for the finding to be made public. As a result, anyone in the world can now access a copy online and the details of how to do so are at the back of this book.

\*

Call it destiny, or maybe the Universal scales of justice in action, but Jim became great friends with another multiple myeloma patient, Henry Jolson OAM. It was Gaynor Wheatley who first introduced them and, despite walking very different paths in life, Jim and Henry liked each other from the outset. Henry was a lawyer, not our favourite profession, and in fact was Queen's Counsel. A highly intelligent, articulate, genuinely compassionate man, Henry was also a humanitarian who was highly respected professionally and personally. One could not help but like Henry.

Jim and Henry met regularly for lunch, usually in the legal sector of the city. One day, Henry told Jim that he'd invited a friend and colleague to join them, who also had myeloma. That colleague was none other than former state coroner Graeme Johnstone, the man who had granted an inquest into William's death and to whom I had addressed countless letters. Graeme had stepped aside as state coroner in 2007, right in the middle of William's inquest, presumably due to ill health. Suddenly, so much became clear: why the investigation at first proceeded swiftly, then appeared to stall for a long time. Jim, Graeme and Henry met regularly for lunches in the city, calling themselves The Blood Brothers, and Jim liked Graeme immensely. It was during one of those lunches that Jim commented to Graeme that his role as state coroner must have been incredibly stressful. Jim told me Graeme's response and I have never forgotten it. Graeme said that he loved his work and felt privileged to be in a position that enabled him to help make a positive difference to the lives of so many people whilst carrying out his duties.

Graeme was the first of The Blood Brothers to pass away and I was deeply saddened when he died. I am eternally grateful to Graeme Johnstone for granting William an inquest, for giving our baby boy a voice by allowing us to speak on his behalf, and have never forgotten his words.

*

Two-thousand and nine was a hectic year of highs and lows. Jim was working and travelling interstate with Cotton Keays & Morris. Our family life which, like most families, normally revolved around school, work and social activities was now dictated by Jim's health at the time. The nature of the disease and the treatment meant that Jim would be doing well, and life would be relatively normal for an extended period of time, until he caught an infection. His immune system, which was compromised by the combination of severe chemotherapy from the stem cell transplant and the multiple myeloma, was not able to fight off a cold or a flu like a healthy person's would. For Jim, a virus would almost inevitably mean a hospital admission and intravenous antivirals, antibiotics and antifungals to do what his body could not do for itself.

I became used to managing the sudden crises, which more often than not occurred late at night. The logistics of arranging for the girls to be looked after in the middle of the night and notifying Russell and Darryl (who would need to modify any gigs to 'Cotton & Morris') was the least of my worries. The hardest part was getting Jim to hospital. The haematologist had told us from the outset that Jim must go immediately to the emergency department at the first sign of fever. Jim never did and would try to hide the fact that he was becoming ill. The first time it happened, I, like Jim, hoped that he would be able to fight it off on his own. The delay meant that, by the time he went to hospital, Jim was desperately ill and had a longer hospital stay and recovery time.

After that, I became adept at noticing the early signs of a fever. Jim, however, would deny he was unwell and refuse to let me take his temperature. I reminded him of what the doctors said last time about getting early treatment, but he would only dig his heels in harder and refuse to go to hospital. Each time, I would reason with him that the best time to go to the hospital was during the day while the girls were at school. Treated early enough, he might even be back home on the same day. Nevertheless, Jim's condition would continue to deteriorate, but he would refuse to let me drive him to hospital or to call an ambulance. He would lie on the lounge shivering and sweating, face flushed bright red, calling for Panadol and more water, all the time refusing to go.

The worst part about this situation was that Holly and Bonnie could see and hear it all, too. The whole, awful situation would end only when I decided to call an ambulance. Jim would then forbid me to call the ambulance, often becoming angry at me, before finally allowing himself to be helped out to the car. Seeing Jim so desperately sick and feverish was distressing and confronting to witness, but it could have been avoided had he gone to the hospital earlier. Every time.

It was a pattern that would continue for the rest of his life and created years of unnecessary conflict and crisis in what was already an incredibly stressful situation. It affected not just Jim but the girls and me, too. Once we got him to hospital, Jim would receive the round-the-clock care and treatment he needed, but Holly, Bonnie and I would be left distressed and limp with exhaustion from days of worry. I write in more depth about the course of Jim's illness and treatment, and its effect on our family, in my second book. For now, I have mentioned this ongoing situation to provide some context for what is to come later in this one.

Throughout the years before and since William's death and Jim's diagnosis, the girls had continued with Highland dancing. The dancing community had rallied around us and were like family. Sarah Adams was not only an amazing dance teacher, she and her family were our friends and provided a safe, caring and stable environment in which Holly and Bonnie could socialise, dance, travel and have fun.

The inaugural Lyons Festival of Dance Competition was on Saturday, 13 June 2009, on what would have been the birthday of

Jim's mum, Nancy. Jim and I were thrilled that Sarah had allowed us to donate a trophy in William's name. This was to be the first time that the William Keays Cup, a perpetual trophy for the Male Dancer of the Day, would be awarded. We had all just gotten over a dose of swine flu. Jim was still very weak, so he stayed home. Bonnie was competing and I was on the door, taking admissions, and I wondered which young man would be taking Billy's trophy home that day.

I'll never forget the first time I saw Adam. I looked up from the ticket book to see a dark-haired boy standing before me, smiling straight at me. I felt like I knew him and hoped immediately that he would be the winner of Billy's trophy. Later, as I got to know Adam and his family, I learned that Adam was thinking exactly the same thing! My heart was bursting when, later that day, I walked forward to shake Adam's hand and present him with the William Keays Cup.

Adam and his family opened their hearts to our family, including William. Their presence in my life continues to be a precious gift. It has been my privilege to watch that beautiful, bright, smiling boy grow into the responsible, handsome, loving man he is today. Adam is now married and he and his wife are themselves proud parents. When I see Adam, I don't confuse him with William, but I do think of William – of what he might have done at Adam's age – and feel in my heart that he is as proud of Adam as I am.

## Chapter Fourteen

# Somebody Loves You

*"Meditate. Live purely. Be quiet.
Do your work with mastery. Like the moon, come out
from behind the clouds! Shine."*
*~ Buddha*

Since our first overseas trip to the UK some fifteen years ago, we had travelled at least every second year, sometimes yearly, to visit Nancy and Sam in the Lake District. It was early in the new millennium when Jim's natural mother, Nancy, left this world and we continued to take regular family holidays to spend time with Sam, and Jim's family. Sam was a doting grandad to Holly and Bonnie, and they adored him in return. He'd spent most of his life utterly devoted to Nancy and now he was alone on the other side of the world.

After Nancy's death, we applied to Australian immigration for his previously granted residency status to be reinstated, but it was refused because he was not Jim's natural father. We were all devastated. Sam had always enjoyed walking for miles every day, delighting in taking me with him when we were in the Lakes and showing me paths to the most breathtaking views. Lately, though, he had stopped walking and was not getting out much. The doctor had prescribed steroids and he was taking them, which made my heart sink. We were worried about him and, in 2009, we were overdue to see Sam, but international travel for any length of time was something that Jim could not do anymore. Apart from the increased risk of infection, he needed to be near the hospital. We decided that I would go to see Sam for a short mid-year holiday with Bonnie. Holly was in high school and missing classes for holidays was no longer an option, so she remained home with Jim. Bonnie and I spent a magic summer's fortnight in England and Scotland and, by the time we said farewell, it was obvious that Sam felt happier and more rejuvenated. Watching Sam's beloved face, waving goodbye as we drove away, I felt torn. I wanted to spend more time with him, to make sure he was really okay, but Jim and Holly also needed me back home.

Looking back, I'm glad that we took that time to be with Sam. Holly had years of happy memories with Sam, but Bonnie had only just reached the age to retain memories. It was in December that we received a phone call to say that Sam had been taken to hospital by ambulance. He'd had a heart attack. He told me later that he'd spent what seemed like hours in the hallway outside his apartment, clinging to the railing with his elbow hooked around it, in the most intense and frightening pain. He knew only that if he laid down or fell down, he'd be dead, so he stayed exactly where he was. Sam was alone in hospital and needed family to be there.

A few days before Christmas, I was on the plane to Manchester, flying into weather such as I'd never known in my life. My friend Isabelle reported from across the English Channel in France, "It's minus 10°C at night and the weather forecast is horrible... snow, snow, everywhere... car crashes... traffic stopped..."

As the plane descended, everything was a greyish white. It was daylight when I arrived, but, by the time I was through immigration and collected the hire car, it was dark. It was also bitterly cold and I drove out of the carpark into, without exaggeration, a genuine blizzard. This Gold Coast girl had never even driven in snow before, let alone a blizzard in northwest England at night.

The M6 northbound is usually a four-lane motorway but not on this night. This night, it was a couple of lanes of tyre tracks in slushy, dark snow and, once the streetlighting of Manchester was left behind, it soon narrowed to a single track. The traffic moved slowly into the wind, which drove the heavy snow straight at the windscreen. Windscreen wipers working furiously, I stayed as close as I dared to the lorry ahead of me, following its tracks through the darkness. The further north I drove, the more the traffic thinned out. People were getting off the roads. On the plane, I'd planned to drive straight to the hospital to see Sam, but I knew now I'd be lucky to make it to the safety of his home.

My relief at seeing the Lakeland exit sign was short-lived as it soon became apparent that there was less traffic on the A road, which meant more snow on the road. I slowed right down and concentrated on keeping the wheels on the tracks through the snow. Once past the market town, things got scary. The road beneath was a two-lane road with ditches and drystone walls on either side, but that night it was only one barely discernible track in the snow. Although I couldn't see the drystone walls and ditches under banks of snow, I knew they were there and stayed mindful of not skidding on black ice and ending up in them. The road snaked and climbed through the isolated countryside with no street lighting. I was the only one silly enough to be on the road, which was scary but also a relief as I didn't fancy having to reverse through the snow to let another car pass.

Finally, I crested the hill into the village. I'd never seen it in the snow before and it looked magical, like a Christmas card. My friend, Jayne, and Sam's neighbour, Lyn, had been into Sam's tiny flat to ensure the heating was on, putting fresh linen on the bed for me and some food in the fridge. I called the hospital to let Sam know I'd arrived safely and would be over to see him tomorrow. Then I called Jim to let him know, too. After that, I showered and fell into bed, but, of course, I had adrenaline pumping through my body after hours of driving in a blizzard so I couldn't sleep. My body was still on Australian time, too. Jetlag is something I'm used to and I knew it would catch up with me eventually. I lay there thinking that I couldn't believe I'd be on the other side of the world from my kids at Christmas.

The next day began with a shovel and a great workout, digging the car out of the snow and ice that had covered it overnight. I'd parked it on the street and it was so deep in solid ice that it was going nowhere. It would have taken me all day if a young boy and his dad hadn't been kind enough to help me. He dug tyre tracks, enough to get it moving, then I was away on the hour-long drive to the hospital. The snowplough had been through, spreading salt whilst clearing the road, but I was always mindful of the peril that is black ice. Lakeland is the most beautiful scenery I have ever seen and now the pale sun was making everything sparkle like diamonds.

Sam was happy to see me, but I saw immediately that he was far from well. I spoke with the doctors and the hospital. He would not be well enough to go home for quite some time. I was concerned that he was so far away from his home and friends and began working with the hospital to arrange for Sam to be transferred to a smaller hospital closer to home, but this would take time.

I had planned to cook Christmas lunch for Lyn and myself then drive Lyn down to see Sam. Aunt Elsie, now widowed, was snowed in on her side of the lake with the road inaccessible, but we spoke daily on the phone. I'd also been invited to spend Christmas night with the family who came to my rescue on the first morning and got my car on the road, but, unfortunately, I caught a gastro bug, which meant spending my first white Christmas alone in bed. Sam and I spoke on the phone and I spoke with Jim and the girls in Australia. It was a strange, lonely feeling, being so far away from my family at Christmas. The girls would have been beside themselves with excitement to see a white Christmas in the village and I wished they could have been there to experience it.

The bug passed, and I resumed the morning routine of getting the snow off my car and on the road to the hospital to spend time with Sam. It was a time of long heart-to-heart talks, some telling of jokes, storytelling, reminiscing and holding hands. Sam spoke a lot about Jim's family history and about his own life growing up in Scotland, about Jim's mother and their life together. I knew he was passing down to me as much information as he could because he knew he was not long for this world.

In the evenings, Jayne and I would walk down the road to the pub for dinner. Jayne lived in the same complex as Sam, but she was more my age than Sam's and we had become good friends over the years. Sometimes, I'd walk up to the village, which looked like fairyland as it was dark by 4.00 pm. After doing my shopping, I'd stop into one of Sam's and my favourite establishments for mulled wine and French onion soup before walking back home. The snow crunched beneath my feet, the air was crisp and smelled of woodsmoke, the village church bells called everyone to early service.

Sam's hospital transfer was on hold as he was not progressing as well as hoped. Each day, he seemed a little frailer. I'd only been there a week when Jim asked me when I was coming back home. He said he wasn't coping with the girls and I was needed there. Jim knew that Sam was not improving as we spoke on the phone every night. I was worried about Sam and wanted to see him well enough to move to the nearby hospital before leaving.

I felt torn between my love for my husband and daughters, my concern for their wellbeing, and my love and concern for Sam, who loved me as a daughter and had no-one but me. I reminded Jim that I had been with him every time he went to hospital and that Sam had nobody else. What if he died after I left? Jim had an ongoing illness, but he was not facing imminent death. I offered to make arrangements for my family or friends to come and help out at home, but Jim was adamant that he needed me to come home now, even going so far as to say that my place was at home with him and the girls.

On New Year's Eve, I visited Sam for the last time, confirming with the hospital the final arrangements for Sam to be moved closer to home. I wore my new, cherry red jumper that I'd bought in the village and Sam smiled at me with a glint in his eye that had been missing for a while. Sitting beside him, I asked him what he thought of my new jumper.

"My dear," he said in his familiar, Scottish brogue that I adored, "If I was 20 years younger, Jim wouldn't stand a chance!"

We sat and talked into the night, something I'd not done before as I tried to be off the icy country roads before nightfall. Sam kept telling me I should go, but I didn't want to, and I knew he didn't really want me to go, either. I didn't want to leave this loyal, dignified, honourable man whom I loved dearly and who loved me and our family in return. It was in this very same hospital that Sam sat with Jim's mum, Nancy, as she spoke her last words and held her as she died. He deserved better than to be left alone and sick.

Eventually, there was no more putting off my departure. We'd said our goodbyes and I turned around for one last look as I walked out the door. He lay there, looking stoically straight ahead, not at me, but his right arm was bent at the elbow with his forearm straight up and palm facing forward in a rigid farewell. It looked just like an illustration from an Uncle Arthur bedtime story from my childhood. In the story, a very sick little boy in hospital asks his friend to prop up his hand with a pillow so that the angels will know to come and get him in the night. The next morning, the friend finds the boy dead, his hand propped up just like Sam's. My heart felt heavy with sadness.

Back at Sam's place, I packed my bag and joined the neighbours downstairs for drinks, dancing and supper. Just before midnight, three pieces of coal and some whiskey were shoved into my hands and I was hustled out the door into the snow to wait, shivering and alone, for the church bells to finish chiming. Then the door opened and I was greeted with smiling faces wishing me Happy New Year as mine was the first foot through the door for 2010. The tradition of 'first footing' is still common in Scotland and Cumbria borders Scotland so Cumbrians will often 'first foot', too. To bring good luck for the New Year, a dark-haired stranger carrying coal and whiskey should be the first person to cross the threshold after midnight. This year, it was me! I sang 'Auld Lang Syne', then said my farewells before jumping in the car and setting off for Manchester airport, all the while, my heart and thoughts were with Sam.

It was a full moon on 1 January 2010. The Lakeland fells were blanketed in snow, but it was a different world from the last time I'd driven this way. The huge full moon was bright, icy blue, and so was everything around me. All was still and the sky was crystal clear with millions of stars twinkling like diamonds against the deepest royal blue. Once again, I had the road to myself and the snow-covered hillsides, trees and farm buildings gleamed with the same icy blue as the moon that hung like a disc in the night sky.

Sam died in hospital early in January and, less than a fortnight after I returned home, I was on a plane back to Manchester. I was numb at times, at others angry. I was angry that Sam had died alone, angry that Jim had insisted I return home and angry with myself for not standing up to him and staying. I cried a lot. My first task was to go straight to the hospital, collect Sam's things and arrange for his body to be released from the morgue to the undertaker. The thought of Sam dying alone in hospital, his body lying in the hospital morgue, waiting for his family to claim it, broke my heart.

The weather had cleared and Aunt Elsie was no longer snowbound so I drove over to see her. Sam's death had hit her hard as Elsie was now the last of that generation of Jim's family. Over a pot of tea and fruit cake, she confided that it was hard being the last one left living when all her family and friends had died, but Elsie was a strong, independent woman to the end and never one to wallow in self-pity.

I organised Sam's funeral and liaised with his solicitors on Jim's behalf. I chose his best suit, putting a lot of care into choosing the perfect shirt and tie for him. I packed his underwear, socks and singlet and took them all to the undertakers. They called me when he was ready to be viewed and I walked up to sit with him a while. Just like William, his spirit had long since passed from the shell of his body and I knew he was with his beloved Nancy, at last. I wondered if our Billy was with them. Sam's funeral was heartbreakingly small for such a wonderful man. Like Elsie, he was one of the last of his family and friends. On the day, I picked up Lyn and we followed the hearse to the crematorium, via the street where Sam and Nancy had lived so he could pass by their home one last time. I remember watching the flower arrangement that I'd ordered on behalf of Holly and Bonnie bobbing along on top of Sam's coffin all the way there. Elsie met us at the crematorium, and I delivered my eulogy along with messages from Jim and the girls. I'd booked a table at our favourite place in the village and hosted a small wake for Sam there. Then I cleaned out the fridge, tidied the flat, put out the garbage and locked it up before heading back to the airport and home to Melbourne.

Later that year, I would return to clean out the flat and settle Sam's affairs. There was one thing left to do and that was to pick up Sam's ashes, which had been sitting at the undertakers since his cremation, awaiting collection. Sam had left no instructions for his final resting place and Jim had no preference. I spoke with Elsie and Jayne at length about various places that Sam had enjoyed, but, in the end, I chose a beautiful spot high in the Lakeland fells. With views in all directions, it looks over Grizedale Forest, where Uncle Bill had been head forester, and many of the places where Sam loved to walk.

*

Back in Melbourne, life resumed… It was almost seven years since William's death and I had not yet had the chance to fully grieve. Life kept delivering one blow after another, lurching continually from one crisis to another. Everything was life or death, it seemed, and everyone in my life depended on me to keep things afloat.

I kept waiting for a window of opportunity when I could schedule some time to grieve into my diary, but it never came. The scream that had been inside me since William's death had never come out, but it was there, waiting for the chance to erupt. The more I tried to make everything right and better for everyone else, the higher the bar was set and the more they expected from me.

My life was lived in loving care and service of my family, but who was looking after me? Who was there for me? My husband, lover and best friend had disappeared the moment he'd begun taking the steroids and cocktail of pharmaceuticals that were the medical protocol for multiple myeloma. Prescription drugs are no different from illicit drugs in terms of side effects. No longer my loyal, dependable ally and partner in love and life, in private, he was increasingly angry, antagonistic and resentful. Sometimes, it felt like he wanted to destroy me. It was yet another huge grief for me but not one I could openly discuss, out of loyalty to my husband.

Over twenty years of living with Jim, of loving him and knowing him in mind, body and spirit more intimately than any other person on the planet, meant that I knew for certain the way he was behaving now was not him. This was *not* my husband. It was the drugs. I felt like I was on the edge of a breakdown and knew I needed help, but the psychologists I'd been seeing couldn't give me the healing I needed. I needed to find a way to support myself through Jim's illness, to be my own best friend in order to be the best I could be, to support my husband and our daughters through what was to come.

I didn't know much about meditation, but the word kept popping up in the most unexpected places and I started to wonder about it. One day, I read an article in the local rag that the Gawler Foundation was starting meditation classes nearby. The Gawler program offered a lifestyle-based, integrative approach to complementary and conventional cancer treatment, of which mindfulness meditation was an important part, and suddenly, I felt compelled to contact them and picked up the phone. I wasn't a cancer patient, but, yes, I was told I could still attend classes. It felt right and I enrolled for the eight-week course immediately.

The classes were small and it was immediately apparent that the teacher had an extraordinary depth of experience in supporting and guiding people in their meditation practice. So began my path to healing. From the very first class, I felt different, lighter, clearer. I'd spent so many years feeling so incredibly, horribly bad inside that the immediate lightening and clarity within was a revelation. Dutifully, at first, I sat every day and meditated. It wasn't always easy. My life was still busy and I had to work out a way to fit an hour a day that was just for me into our family schedule. There were still constant health crises and Jim was ambivalent about my meditation practice, referring to it as my 'medication'. At first, most days were a struggle with my mind running off in its own direction, churning over the myriad problems and worries of life. Sometimes, I felt like I was lucky to get a few moments of inner stillness, but I kept sitting down for an hour every day and continued to attend the weekly classes because, even if only for a few moments, that exquisite inner peace and joy was worth it.

One day, I walked into the class as usual and greeted the small group of ladies. There was nothing to indicate what would occur, no warning, nothing different from any other day. We sat and listened to our teacher as she explained the meditation technique we would be doing that day. It was a way of forgiving, of finding true peace through forgiveness. I knew immediately who I had to forgive, but could I do it? Could I really, truly and utterly forgive that which seemed unforgiveable? Closing my eyes, we began a small practice of the meditation but, immediately, I felt something almost inexplicable. It was like the elusive door was very near, the door that I'd been searching for from the moment William died. There was an energy flowing around and through me such as I'd never known and the sheer power of what was on the other side of that door made my body tremble and caused tears to rain down my cheeks from beneath my closed eyes. As the short practice concluded, I felt embarrassed. Sniffling, I scrabbled for a tissue to blow my nose.

Quietly, our teacher checked in with each of us as to how we were feeling and, when it was my turn to speak, I began to cry again as I explained that I wanted to try to forgive the obstetrician and midwife. Then, out of nowhere, the words tumbled from my mouth, "Can I use this meditation to forgive myself?"

Until that moment, I hadn't consciously thought it, but my subconscious knew the truth. In order to truly forgive, I needed to forgive myself, too, for not trusting my intuition and my own inner guidance. Here, at last, I was being shown the way to do that.

Closing my eyes once again, I dropped back into the meditation. There was no struggling to reach anywhere or any state of being. I was right where I needed to be, as though this moment in space and time had been waiting for me to arrive. Something was waiting for me on the other side of forgiveness, a bright light and energy so immensely powerful that my body trembled before it, and tears streamed from beneath my closed eyelids.

With each forgiveness, the light expanded and drew closer with a pulsing energy until, finally, once I had forgiven myself there was nothing left between us. I looked straight into the light, sobbing and shaking, because I knew I was looking at William in spirit. He was a pure, blindingly bright light, filling my vision and radiating a loving energy more powerful than my mind could comprehend but my heart and spirit knew his immediately.

"Can you ever forgive me?" I asked silently.

An enormous wave of loving energy swept around and through me as the words resonated, "You know there's nothing to forgive."

Then came the words that I hadn't dared to hope for, "Now, can we cuddle?"

I opened my heart and arms wide immediately and the light changed shape at the centre, the form of a baby emerging and floating into my waiting arms, the enormous light enfolding us both like wings. Mother and child cocooned in pure light and love. Finally, at long last, my baby was in my arms, cradled to my heart and we sat like that, our spirits loving each other as I wept in gratitude and joy. My bleeding heart began to heal, and my arms were no longer empty. My heart's desire had been waiting for me all along, waiting for me to put myself into a place where William's spirit could meet me, and when I did, he was right there.

Learning meditation was one of the best, most loving decisions I've made in my life. In finding my own path to healing and inner peace, I became a better, stronger, more loving person, not only for my family but also for myself. I gained insight into and compassion for the fearful behaviours of the ego, the clarity to recognise them and the strength to make difficult decisions for the greater good of all concerned. In forgiving others, I released myself from any energetic attachment to them.

*

By late 2012, Jim and I had separated. Even now, writing those words, I struggle to believe it, and the story of how our marriage had come to that point is a book of its own. Jim had become increasingly focused on money. He was no longer the same man whose first thoughts when faced with a terminal diagnosis had been for my financial security. In the five years since, his narrative was increasingly bitter and resentful. Most distressing of all, he would say things like, "I don't want some other guy getting all *my* money." When, I wondered, had our family home and business – all that we'd sacrificed and worked for together as a team, all for one and one for all – become Jim's and not ours? It was as though there was an evil entity whispering words of poison in his ear. As it turned out, there was, but that story is for another time. Yet, despite the machinations of self-serving others, our true love did not die, and in our hearts, nor did our marriage. Throughout the year between separation and our financial settlement, Jim persisted in his adversarial stance, but, once the money was settled and I'd let Jim have his win, I was still fronting up each day with a loving heart just as I always had. It didn't take long for Jim to realise that there was no reason for continued antagonism as I presented no threat to him at all. In fact, I never had. One day, I went round to Jim's and noticed the same letter sitting on the coffee table that I had at my house. It was a letter officially confirming our divorce.

"Oh look! You've got one of those, too!" I said wryly.

Jim reached over from the couch, picked up the paper with his fingertips like it was toxic and flicked it towards me. It landed on the floor at my feet.

"Burn it!" he said. "Get rid of it, I don't want to know about it."

From the day we separated until the end of Jim's life, we never lived more than ten minutes away from each other. Jim knew, because I never stopped reminding him, that I would always be there for him in sickness and in health. I know many friends were confused by our separation and subsequent divorce because, clearly, there was no lack of love between us, and we still spent a lot of time together. Having separate residences meant that, when Jim's behaviour became unacceptable on steroid days, I no longer had to engage or pacify to keep peace in the home. I would simply bid him farewell and leave, returning to the sanctuary of my own space. If Jim was at my house and began to get antagonistic, I did not hesitate to ask him to leave. It didn't take long for us to settle into an amicable understanding and enjoy our time together without the angst. Most importantly, our two daughters witnessed our continued love for each other and for them.

In reality, I was still Jim's primary carer, but I never took a cent of government monies for caring for my husband and partner because I was not caring for him out of duty or for financial gain. Our finances had been settled in court and, as far as I was concerned, that part was over and done. Jim would always be the love of my life and father of our children, and I cared for him because I wanted to. I cared for him because I love him.

*

In mid 2013, Bonnie and I had just returned from a trip to the UK. Tired and jetlagged, I fell into bed only to wake with a jolt in the middle of the night. Turning on the bedside lamp, I looked at the wardrobe on the wall opposite. On the top shelf, hidden at the back, was the tiny box that contained William's ashes. For ten years, it had been with me, always close to me because what do you do with a baby's ashes? He'd never been anywhere, never known anything but the safety of my body until his horrific death. I wouldn't put him alone in the cold ground of a strange cemetery. It was the only thing I ever worried about when I left the house. I worried that, if there was a burglary, thieves might prise open the box and scatter the ashes. The girls knew that William's ashes were to be scattered with mine in a place of their choosing when I died, but, until then, the tiny box of his mortal remains stayed close to my bed.

That night, I had an epiphany that woke me from the deepest sleep and, this time, I wasn't going to second guess it. William's ashes needed to be with Sam's, his grandad who loved him, until my time came to join them. Not only did it feel right, it felt urgent. I knew this feeling and it was not to be ignored. The next day, I could hardly wait to tell Jim and went over to see him as soon as I woke. Although it was entirely my call, I wanted to be sure that Jim was okay with our son being laid to rest on the other side of the world. I told him about the feeling that had woken me in the night and how important it felt to me.

Jim looked at me quietly, then he said hesitantly, "Do you think it would be a good place for me, too?"

Tears sprang to my eyes and my heart clenched. Our ESP, that psychic connection that we'd had since 1988, had gone missing, on and off, for the past few years, but I'd hoped he would say this.

"I think it would be the perfect place for you, Darling," I said. "We'll all be together there in the end, and I can't think of a more beautiful place in the world for us to spend eternity."

That afternoon, I booked a flight and within two weeks I was flying back into Manchester, picking up a car and heading north on the M6 for The Lakes. I'd obtained all the necessary permissions and paperwork to carry William's ashes on board with me so there would be no issue. William stayed close by me the whole way, inside my carry-on bag in the locker over my head and beside me on the passenger seat of the car. It felt right. I was taking my son home.

As the name suggests, the Lake District is full of water and that is because it rains there… a lot. I spent a couple of days catching up with friends, getting over the long trip whilst waiting for the rain to clear. One fine day, I opened the box containing William's ashes for the first time and transferred them into a lightweight, sealed container that I'd brought with me for this purpose. I'd been told by the funeral director that the original seals could become difficult to break after several years, so I gently prised it open in my room. Ever so carefully, I poured every last grain into the new container with a wider opening and closed the lid.

Then I took a walk with my dear friend Mick, the same walk we took together in 2010 when I carried Sam's ashes up a Lakeland fell and laid him to rest in one of the most beautiful places I know. Today I carried the mortal remains of my baby son along with a posy of fresh flowers and sprigs of holly, all picked from the garden where Nancy and Sam had lived. It had taken me almost ten years to come to this point, but I now felt at peace knowing that my Billy's remains would be safe forevermore with his grandad. We found the spot at the top of the steep hill that held Sam's ashes and would now forever hold my baby's remains too. Mick stood quietly by, making sure I was not disturbed. He took photographs for the family and had my back, giving me silence and space. He was comfortable with my tears and later, as we sat to take in the view, we smiled and hoped that we'd never have to do this again.

The next day, I enjoyed lunch and a chat with Mick in the village before driving to the nearest market town, where I purchased a lovely pair of lightweight, waterproof, plum, leather hiking shoes with burgundy laces. The purchase was prompted by the previous day's walk to the top of the hill with William and the subsequent descent that saw me almost slip and land on my behind more times than I cared to count. From time to time, I would meet the curious, gentle eyes of a Herdwick, the hardy and sure-footed breed of sheep that is native to Cumbria. Something had to be done about my footwear. So, when I returned to the place at the top of the hill the next day, I was channelling a Herdwick sheep, all nimble-footed and sure of step. When I arrived at the summit, to my dismay, I found yesterday's floral tribute in complete disarray! Who would do such a thing? Then I realised, the hollow in between the roots of the tree that had seemed like a perfect natural vase for the flowers was, in fact, the front door of a local resident. This being the Lake District and home of Beatrix Potter, it had to be either Mrs. Tiggy-Winkle, Samuel Whiskers or maybe the star of the show... Peter Rabbit! I sat beneath the tree and laughed and laughed. For three years, this little being had been walking over Sam on a nightly basis and now it would be walking over Billy as well! He was going to love it!

The next day I was packed and ready for the drive south, but first I would climb the hill once more to say farewell to the boys. Stopping in the village, I bought white roses to leave for Billy and Sam and enjoyed a surprisingly good coffee. In our travels over the years, Jim and I had often lamented the lack of a good espresso anywhere in the UK. No longer the case, I smiled as I thought of Jim, who would be fast asleep in Melbourne, and wished I could call him to tell him about the coffee. I would speak with him later because the day was special for us. It was on this date, one night 25 years ago, that I had walked with Snezana up to Jim's front door and first met my future husband and father of our three children, Holly, Bonnie and William.

*"There are places on this Earth where I have felt so close to Heaven that I could almost touch it, hear it, see it."*

So it was on our 25th meeting anniversary that I found myself lying flat on my back in soft, green grass, high on a fell in the English Lake District, contemplating the sky through the branches of a very special tree. I thought of Jim on the other side of the world. I thought of the young woman I'd been a quarter of a century ago, with all my hopes and dreams of international travel and romance. I'd lived them all with Jim by my side, just not in the ways I'd expected. Back then, I could never have imagined I'd be lying here, near the place where I'd scattered the ashes of our baby son, Billy, and his grandad, Sam. Part of me marvelled that I could feel so at peace in my heart. No longer bereft, my heart overflowed with gratitude and I felt blessed beyond measure. Gratitude for the abundance of love in my life. In its truest form, love is the only part of us that never dies, the only part of our lifetime that is eternal. To be so truly, deeply loved and to love in return, is the greatest gift of all.

## AFTERWORD

True Love never dies, so this is not the end of the story. Until a couple of years ago, the title of this book was always *Angel in My Arms*. What began as a story written to help grieving parents, changed shape almost of its own accord and became something far greater. Our children, Holly, Bonnie and William, were born out of great love and William's story could not be told without first telling the story of that love.

Written with the intention of sharing knowledge – a sharing of information that I wished I'd known at the time – this book began as William's story, what happened and what I learned along the way. Life did not stop unfolding, though. Jim's cancer diagnosis and long illness overlapped with William's story and I kept on wishing that I'd known beforehand what I had to learn the hard way, always on the back foot. The story of my life, the lessons learned from dealing with cancer in the family, could not be abbreviated without losing the messages that might help so many others.

I kept writing and the book kept getting longer . Then one day I realised that it had to be two separate books. 'Because I Love You' is the song title of the timeless Masters Apprentices classic from 1971, written by Jim Keays and Doug Ford, and recorded in the magical Abbey Road Studios in London. It was the perfect and obvious name for this book. All of the chapter names are song titles written by Jim Keays. If you haven't heard them before, I urge you to jump onto the website and explore www.jimkeays.com.

I am delighted to share that I am currently writing my second book, with the working title of *Angel in My Arms!* If you would like a preview of what's to come, you can find an excerpt from it at the end of this book, which I hope you'll enjoy.

With love and gratitude,
Karin

# APPENDIX

**Coroner's finding**

Today, everyone in the world can access a copy of the coroner's finding online at: www.coronerscourt.vic.gov.au

Click on the drop-down menu titled **Inquests & Findings**, then click on **Findings**. When the **Search Listing** box appears, enter William's case number, 3683, or his name, William Grant Keays. Scroll to the bottom of the page to click on William's name in the Findings list.

# REFERENCES

Spencer, M.K. & MacLennan, A. (2001). How long does it take to deliver a baby by emergency Caesarean section? Department of Obstetrics' and Gynaecology, Adelaide University, South Australia. doi: 10.1111/j.1479-828x.2001.tb01287.x.

## ABOUT THE AUTHOR

Karin Keays was born and raised in the tropical state of Queensland, Australia, and grew up in Burleigh Heads on the Gold Coast, only minutes' walk from one of the world's most beautiful surf beaches. Karin attended Burleigh State School and graduated from Miami High School. Her weekends and school holidays were mostly spent at the beach or with her sister and cousins at the family's banana plantation, set amongst pristine rainforest and natural waterfalls in Currumbin Valley.

At 23, Karin travelled to Melbourne and fell in love with Australian music great, Jim Keays. Jim was singer/songwriter in the legendary Masters Apprentices, an influential band who consistently pushed boundaries in their art and performance, the quality of which earned them their rightful place in the ARIA Hall of Fame. Together, Karin and Jim were partners in life and in business for over 25 years. As co-owner and administrator of Masters Apprentices Pty. Ltd., Karin acquired an in-depth knowledge of all aspects of the Australian music industry.

As Jim's soul mate, it was Karin who encouraged Jim to pick up his long-neglected brushes and rediscover his love of watercolour painting after they married. Relishing the joy of his return to one of his earliest mediums of artistic expression, Jim was prolific, and he created more than 150 watercolour paintings and drawings, which he bequeathed to Karin before his passing in 2014. In 2016, Karin laid the groundwork, preparing and carefully choosing Jim's art pieces in what was to be the first-ever gallery exhibition entitled 'The Secret Life of a Rock Legend'. This was successfully showcased in Melbourne, at Hawthorn Studio and Gallery.

After Jim's passing, Karin resumed her career in Business and Logistics. In 2019, Karin was appointed Manager of the Estate of her late husband. As Director of Masters Apprentices Pty. Ltd., she manages all aspects of Jim's career including his music and visual recordings, artwork and intellectual property.

Karin is also a qualified facilitator of mindfulness meditation, professional speaker and an advocate for holistic health and wellbeing. Karin feels privileged to be able to share the knowledge gained from her depth of experience, in the hope that doing so may help other women and families navigate their way through the overwhelm of grief after the death of a loved one and, ultimately, find their own path to reclaiming joy in life.

Encouraged by friends and colleagues who had already moved north, Karin is now based on the beautiful Gold Coast and is delighted to be part of the burgeoning arts and entertainment industry of her hometown. As a talented writer, Karin has once again returned to her passion and love of words as a published author and travel writer.

Karin Keays

[www.karinkeays.com](http://www.karinkeays.com)

[www.jimkeays.com](http://www.jimkeays.com)

# CREDITS

My sincere gratitude to the following people for their approvals and contributions to the publishing of this book:

To Fiona Smith from Contempo Publishing, thank you for taking on my manuscript and bringing my first book to life! I am thrilled to be working with you and already look forward to our next project.

To Alyce Evans and Jennifer Tutty from Studio Legal, thank you for not only having my back but also having your sights set firmly on the road ahead, sweeping aside any rocks and filling any potholes. I love speaking with you two highly intelligent yet compassionate, gorgeous women who really know your stuff. Seriously, I have the best legal team ever!

To Dianna O'Neill from Dianna O'Neill Publicity, thank you for being our amazing publicist and treasured family friend. It's only fitting that we first met on the red carpet! Our family is blessed to have you in our life.

To the Estate of the late Jim Keays, to Doug Ford and to Sony Music Publishing, my sincere gratitude and appreciation for your approval to reference Ford/Keays song titles and lyrics.

To Damian Rinaldi from Sonic Lawyers, thank you for heading our legal team for all music business matters. Your expertise is invaluable, and I thank you for your sage advice on the relevant parts of this book.

To Russell Morris AM, thank you for your wonderful testimonial and for unwittingly making yourself a key character in this book, simply by being our dear friend.

To Gaynor Wheatley, thank you for your beautiful testimonial, for reading my manuscript in one day and for really seeing our darling Billy Keays. You and Glenn were always going to appear in our love story and the story of my life... how could you not? I love that the friendship forged by Glenn and Jim so many years ago, lives on through us.

To Alan Howe, thank you for your insightful testimonial. Your friendship and unfailing support for Jim's work over so many years is deeply appreciated by me, as I know it was by Jim.

To Sahara Herald, thank you, my darling friend, for writing – with no hesitation when asked – the most beautiful, insightful Foreword for my book and for your unswerving love and friendship.

To the authors of *Always a Part of Me. Surviving Childbearing Loss* (published by ABC Books, 2001), Amanda Collinge, Sue Daniel and Heather Grace Jones, thank you for approving my request to reference your book.

To Carmel Egan, my sincere thanks for all of your support and for granting me permission to re-publish your newspaper articles from the *Age*.

To the *Age*, thank you for permitting me to re-publish the articles from the time of William's inquest.

To the Coroners Court of Victoria, thank you all for the unfailing courtesy and willingness to help that you have shown me throughout the Inquest and beyond.

To **Bruce Lee LLC**, thank you for your willingness to consider my request and for so kindly granting permission to publish the quote of Bruce Lee in this book.

The Bruce Lee name, likeness, image likeness and all related indicia are intellectual property of Bruce Lee Enterprises, LLC. All Rights Reserved. www.brucelee.com

To Lorraine Long of Medical Error Action Group, I am almost lost for words… but not quite. You were a light in the darkness all those years ago. When it seemed nobody wanted to listen to my questions and concerns, I happened across you. You listened, you took notes, you made suggestions, but most of all, you knew exactly what I was talking about. Thank you for your permission to quote your words in this book and thank you for your tireless work over so many years, for your commitment to change for the greater good of all.

To Ina May Gaskin and Sarah Culver, thank you for so graciously granting approval to include the quote by Ina May in my book. Reading *Spiritual Midwifery* by Ina May Gaskin was lifechanging for me and I thank you sincerely for your gift to the world.

Thank you to Montsalvat in Eltham VIC, for permitting the cover photograph to be shot in the same location where Jim and I were married and had our wedding photos.

To Andrew Gash (photographer), Fiona Pattinson (makeup, hair and styling), Athina Wilson (concepts and planning) and Martine Gunstone (Hair Styling). With all of my heart, thank you for creating the stunning cover photo for this book. After the many hours of preparation and planning with Fiona and Athina, I will never forget the spine-tingling conclusion of the photo shoot in the gallery at Montsalvat. Jim's voice singing 'Because I Love You' soared through the Great Hall just as it had at our wedding reception 35 years ago. There was magic in the air once again and for this, I thank you, Andrew Gash.

To Sera Bomba, thank you for getting straight off a plane from Paris and doing a beautiful, last minute photo edit for my cover photo! You saved the day!

To Dominic Barbuto from Visible Ink Design, our dear friend for many years, thank you for your love and friendship and for the Karin Keays logo design.

## IN GRATITUDE

To Jim, my darling husband, my soul mate, my champion. For 25 years, you were my knight in shining armour, my lover and my best friend. Our love is written in the stars. Until we meet again, my love, always.

To our beautiful daughters, Holly and Bonnie, divine beings whose unstinting love, support and belief in me has enabled this book to be completed. You are amazing young women of strength and compassion, beautiful both inside and out. You make me so proud to be your mum, every day of my life, and I love both of you with all of my heart.

To William, our beautiful son, thank you with all that I am for the honour of choosing me to be your mummy. I love you with all of my heart.

To all of my wonderful family – Dad, Mum and Trina – thank you for your love, for always being there from the very beginning and for the gift of growing up on the Gold Coast.

To my aunts Valerie and Margaret, women of strength, grace and beauty, you nurtured me as a child and enriched my adult life with your love and friendship. I would not be the woman I am without you.

To all of my uncles, aunts and cousins (of whom there are many), without you my life would be so much smaller and poorer. Thank you. I love being part of our family.

To Nancy and Sam, thank you for opening your hearts to me and being fabulous parents-in-law. The girls and I love you and miss you always.

To Snezana, my soul sister, without you there would have been no Jim, and no Holly, Bonnie and William. It does not bear thinking about! I love you forever and love how we do life together, even when we are half a world apart.

To Sherrin, my beloved, truest and most loyal friend, woman of integrity and compassion. You are my rock, and I don't know how I'd have come this far without you. Thank you with all of my heart, for being a most loved and treasured part of our family.

To Nicki, my sparkling Sagittarian friend with the same shoe size, what times we have shared! Life hasn't always been easy for either of us, but being your friend is effortlessly fun and spiritually enriching all at once. Love you longtime.

To Kelly and Leah, you are the family we choose. Kelly, you have saved my life twice! How can such a debt ever be repaid? We love you both with all of our hearts.

To Russell and Donna Morris, I feel blessed that the decades of love, loyalty and friendship between Russell and Jim has extended to enfold our families. Thank you for your unstinting love, care, friendship and support. My love to you both.

To Cheryl and the late Darryl Cotton, Dazzler left a space that can never be filled. Loved and missed by all who knew him. Cheryl, dear one, how strange it is that we walk this parallel path through life. My love to you always.

To Sahara Herald, Drew and Brad Shepherd, thank you for allowing me to include your story about the loss of your precious Maddie. To Sahara, your beautiful Foreword takes my breath away. My love and respect to you all

To Karyn and Andy Kennedy, thank you for allowing me to tell the story of your beautiful Saoirse. William and Saoirse, their stories are forever entwined and so are ours. With love and respect.

To the team at Ultimate 48 Hour Author for your mentorship, coaching and support. I love being part of your community of authors.

To Terry Davis from VMC Design, thank you for your wonderful work and willingness to help with the early stages of cover design and for being my true friend.

To Dianna O'Neill, Alan Howe, Carmel Egan, Gaynor Wheatley, Tony Healy, Loretta and Michael Rymer, thank you all for your friendship, encouragement, support and willingness to help me get this book published.

To our many wonderful friends, neighbours and community, to everyone who reached out with a helping hand, a hug, a home-cooked meal, looked after our daughters, turned up for our family in times of sorrow and crisis and held space for us, please know you have my eternal gratitude. Your every single act of kindness and compassion helped to build a bridge that saved our family from drowning. You are the good in this world.

My husband was always going to be a hard act to follow. Frankly, I didn't think anyone could or would.

Then, one day, a big, strong man with a big, warm smile to match his enormous heart rode into my life on his gorgeous, white Harley Davidson Heritage Softail called Marilyn Monroe and we fell in love.

To my partner, Michael, I thank you with all of my heart for all your love, encouragement and support in helping me to get this book out into the world in time for William's 21st year.

I love you very much.

Excerpt from –

## ANGEL IN MY ARMS

By
Karin Keays

The inquest was over and all that was left to do was wait for the coroner to hand down her finding. We had been given the final date for hearing of evidence months ahead, so I booked early bird airfares and planned an extra special overseas holiday for our family. Our first stop was four nights in a historic home in Lancashire, then a week in the Lakes District before driving south to the edge of the Cotswolds. From there, we were to travel to Paris where I'd booked three nights in a self-contained apartment in the heart of the City of Light. The pièce de résistance was four nights in the Loire Valley, somewhere Jim and I had never been and always wanted to explore. I'd found a chateau where we had our own suite of rooms and the girls' bedroom was actually in a turret!

We were all worn down by years of grief and having been grist for the mill of the medico-legal system in our pursuit of social justice. My diary through 2007 was a weird mix of family, school, business and travel, mixed amongst inquest dates and legal meetings.

Two-thousand and seven was Bonnie's first year at school. Early in the year, Jim hurt his back playing with Bonnie and it had never really improved. By mid-year, he was coming home from gigs grey and exhausted, sitting on the edge of the lounge rocking back and forward in pain. He was reluctant to see a doctor and, after what we'd just been through with the medical industry, you couldn't blame him. I was concerned about him sitting upright for 24 hours on a long-haul flight to England. In the days before departure, a practitioner told him to have some painkillers that combined codeine and an anti-inflammatory, to help him cope with the plane flight to London.

We were all barely dragging ourselves over the line and onto the plane, spent and numb from living through something that no family should have to. We'd done everything we could for William and now the result was out of our hands and in the hands of the coroner. The girls had lived through it, too, and Holly was showing signs of behavioural changes. Her sunny smile and innately funny nature were rarely to be seen and I was concerned about the dark smudges under her eyes that weren't going away. We'd all become hypervigilant, wondering which direction the next blow was coming from like beaten animals. It was time to go to our happy place and remember how to relax and feel safe again, to laugh and have fun and move forward into learning how to do life after William.

There's a photo of Jim that I took on the plane. He is trying to smile for the photo, but obviously in pain, that greyness around his mouth that had never really gone away is obvious and he's sort of hunched over. Throughout the flight, he couldn't get comfortable no matter how many painkillers he took and sat there rocking backwards and forwards on that long journey. I was worried about him. It was a relief for all of us when we landed in Manchester and picked up the hire car I'd booked before driving to our first B&B in Lancashire.

The owners were lovely people and welcomed us into their historic home. We had the beautifully decorated guest wing to ourselves with two bedrooms, bathroom and lounge room. The bath was a treat, freestanding and deep with a view through a window that took in the valley and hills beyond. Each morning, we would go down for breakfast in the shippon, which is an old cattle shed that was typically attached to traditional farmhouses, before heading out to sightsee. We visited pretty villages, ate at quintessentially English pubs, explored ancient castles and the Forest of Bowland. They were four days of fun, but, for the first time ever, Jim wasn't up to climbing the castle turrets with me to walk the ramparts. He would find a seat or lie on the grass and wait patiently for the girls and me. We were trying hard to keep things happy and fun, but we all knew something was not right. It wasn't like the joyous, carefree holidays that we'd always loved.

From there we drove to the Lakes District to see Sam in our second home. I'd booked a week in a 400-year-old self-catering cottage near the historic village of Hawkshead. My Uncle Maurie and Auntie Valerie were holidaying in England at the time, visiting my cousin, Ben, who was living and working in Newcastle. We'd planned ahead for them to stay with us and have some wonderful memories of that week and treasured photos of Sam and Jim's Aunt Elsie in the stunning cottage garden drinking tea with Valerie and Maurie. There are lovely photos of Ben, a 6-foot 7-inch rugby player, clowning around with the girls on Elsie's front lawn with Coniston Water in the background. Missing from the photos, though, was Jim. He visited Elsie with us, but it wore him out and he had to rest afterwards. The next day, we drove across to North Yorkshire for a family day trip – something we always loved to do. Jim put on a brave face but was subdued and clearly not well. He refused my offer to book a doctor's appointment.

On the drive back across the Pennines, we stopped at a petrol station to refuel and Jim insisted on going into the shop to pay. He wanted to buy some Kendal Mint Cake for Richard Rushton, who had played guitar and managed Cotton Keays & Morris until his retirement. Richard and his lovely wife, Chris, were from Yorkshire and we always brought a supply of Richard's favourite sweet back for him. The memory of Jim hobbling gingerly, like an old man, into the petrol station is one I'll never forget. Something was very wrong, and I was worried.

When we got back to the cottage, Jim put himself to bed and didn't come downstairs for the rest of the week until it was time to get in the car and drive to Oxfordshire, which was completely out of character for my social, gregarious husband. During that week in the Lakes, he stayed in bed shivering feverishly and hardly eating. He still wouldn't see a doctor, insisting he had a virus and just needed to sleep, but as the week drew to a close, Jim was getting worse and feeling nauseous.

I packed the car in readiness for the seven-hour drive to Oxfordshire. The girls were in the back seat of the car ready to go. I did an idiot check of the cottage before waking Jim and helping him down the creaky, narrow stairwell and into the front passenger seat. The sun was shining and it was a beautiful day for a road trip, but the girls and I were subdued and worried about Jim, who spent the whole trip either vomiting into a container or dozing fitfully and moaning in pain at every bump in the road.

During the course of that long drive, Jim had finally agreed with me that he needed to see a doctor. It was late afternoon when we arrived. Jim was exhausted and stayed in the car while I went in to meet our B&B host. We'd all been excited to stay at this farm, deep in the beautiful Oxfordshire countryside on the edge of the Cotswolds. We had our own suite of rooms in the old farmhouse with a balcony and glorious views. Best of all, the lady of the house was a keen horsewoman and offered riding lessons for the girls.

In Britain, B&B guests are usually welcomed on arrival with afternoon tea and a chat with the host before heading to their rooms to rest and freshen up. I explained to the lady that my husband was unwell and needed to go straight to bed. Once Jim was tucked in upstairs, I went downstairs to join the girls for afternoon tea. The lady of the house handed me a list of local doctors and contact numbers and discussed options with me. We both agreed that going to emergency at the main hospital in Oxford was the best plan. I took the girls out to a local pub for dinner, then we all got an early night in readiness for the drive into the city of Oxford.

We spent most of the next day in the emergency department waiting room of the hospital, something that would become a regular part of our lives. We just didn't know it yet. I'd come prepared for a long wait, bringing games, Textas and colouring-in books for the girls. It was boring for them, but they were very patient. I was so proud of them. We all wanted Jim to get better and so we waited and waited. When Jim was called in, the girls and I weren't allowed to go with him so I didn't get to hear what the doctor said. It was frustrating because Jim was so unwell that he probably wasn't taking in everything he was told.

After a while, Jim walked out with a piece of paper and said, "Let's go."

I wanted to know what the doctor said and Jim told me he said that the pain was from his fractured spine and they'd prescribed a stronger dosage of codeine. The vomiting and fever was likely from a virus and would pass.

Jim had actually asked the doctor outright, "What if I have cancer or something?"

The reply was that he would have to be a lot sicker than he was before they would start looking for cancer.

Once again, we got into the car and I drove us back into the countryside. After taking a dose of the new painkillers, Jim went straight back to bed and that is where he stayed. The drugs didn't seem to help as Jim was still moaning in pain and not eating. Despite this, Jim refused to see another doctor and just wanted to stay in bed.

During the day, I would take the girls for day trips to our favourite Cotswold locations. They also had riding lessons from our host, properly kitted out. We have some wonderful memories of that time, but it felt like living a dual life because, whilst I was taking photos and videos of our daughters, my thoughts were with the love of my life. I could see the room where he was lying in bed sick and wanted to be with him, too. A couple of days later, Jim's condition was deteriorating and I made an appointment with a local GP for a second opinion.

It was unusual for me to go against Jim's wishes in anything and he wasn't happy about it. He told me to cancel it, but I stood my ground, pointing out the fact that there was no way he could travel to France in this condition. It was true. He could barely get out of bed to go to the bathroom and hadn't eaten for days.

Early the next morning, we all got in the car and headed in to the village medical practice. Again, I had to remain outside with the girls and when Jim came out, he looked shaken. He told me to drive straight home and, on the way, he filled me in. The doctor had told him that he needed to go back to the hospital in Oxford and present at emergency for further tests. Jim wanted to go home to Australia, but the doctor made it clear that he would have to get on a plane immediately if he was going to do that as he needed urgent medical attention.

I wanted to drive straight to the hospital, but Jim refused, insisting we go back to our accommodation and change our flights. We didn't know what was wrong with him, but Jim was adamant that he wanted to be in Australia if he needed medical treatment. Jim went back to bed and I got on the phone to change the flights and get us all back home ASAP.

Unfortunately, it wasn't that easy, being mid-summer in the UK and peak tourist season, especially for Aussies. The airline was fully booked ex-London for weeks ahead. The quickest way for us to get home would be to go to France and keep our original booking. Jim was far too unwell to even contemplate that option. Still, he refused to go to hospital, becoming increasingly angry with me whenever I tried to discuss it with him.

Compounding the urgency of the situation were the devastating rain and floods of 2007. Whilst we had managed to have some sunny weather on our holiday, we had been hearing about the rain and floods elsewhere in Britain. We had been lucky enough to skip around the bad weather until now, but it was catching up with us fast. To the west, all along the Welsh Marches, the River Severn and her tributaries were bursting their banks and flooding towns, villages and farmland. People and animals were dying. Tens of thousands of people were displaced and headed eastward ahead of the weather to emergency accommodation, including Oxford.

At night, while Jim and the girls slept, I stayed up late calling friends in Australia, trying in vain to pull some strings to get us on a flight. I called the travel insurance company, but there was nothing they could do without Jim first seeing a doctor for a diagnosis and treatment of whatever it was that ailed him. We couldn't stay in the accommodation indefinitely as our rooms were already booked ahead by other guests.

Jim needed to go to hospital, no matter his wishes. It was going to be another difficult conversation in the morning, and I was already exhausted and anxious. Sliding carefully into bed so as not to disturb Jim, I turned out the light and tried to sleep.

I'd left the phone on in case someone from Australia called with news about flights so when it rang, I was half asleep and confused to hear an Australian voice asking to speak with Jim Keays. I asked who was speaking and the man introduced himself as a reporter from a major newspaper. He said he was wanting to get a comment from Jim about Glenn Wheatley's conviction today. I asked him what he meant by that, and he told me that Glenn had been sentenced to 15 months jail.

It felt like I'd dropped into a nightmare in some sort of parallel dimension. Numbly, I told the reporter that we were on a family holiday in the UK, it was the middle of the night and that Jim was unwell. He apologised and I told him that Jim was unaware of what had happened and would have no comment to make anyway.

Hanging up from the call, I lay in the dark thinking. How could it be that Glenn was going to jail? I couldn't get my head around it, couldn't imagine how Glenn, Gaynor and their children must be feeling. My heart ached for them. Beside me, Jim stirred and moaned in pain.

"Who was that?" he croaked.

"It was a reporter wanting a comment from you." I took a breath and continued.

"Darling, he said that Glenn Wheatley is going to jail for 15 months."

In the dark, Jim grunted then moaned and fell back into the semi-comatose state that he'd been in since seeing the GP. I'd noticed a whiff of a strange smell in the room and realised that it was coming from Jim. He'd had a shower before going to the doctor and it wasn't the smell of an unwashed body. I'd never smelled anything like it before, but it was dank and kind of musty. It smelled off and, unbidden, the thought came to me that maybe it was the smell of death.

The world had gone mad. Here we were in the depths of the English countryside, which had always been our happy place. My husband lay beside me, sick and in pain and refusing treatment. On the other side of the world, his longtime friend and fellow Masters Apprentices band member was in jail. Both men, in their own way, had worked tirelessly to build their careers and create a good life for their families. The name of Masters Apprentices was revered and respected, but, here in the darkness with a storm on the way, it seemed like everything they'd built was collapsing around them like a house of cards.

When morning came, the sun was nowhere to be seen and the sky was filled with angry clouds the colour of bruises hanging low in the sky. The air felt ominously still, the calm before the storm. I woke Jim gently and told him that the rains were due to hit the area today and floods were predicted. It was time to go to the hospital, as the GP had advised. Predictably, our discussion began with Jim getting angry with me and refusing to go. I stood my ground and pointed out that we had a small window of opportunity to drive to Oxford and present at the hospital. Jim wasn't well enough to travel to Paris and being so sick in another country where we didn't speak the language was not ideal, anyway. Our booking at the B&B was about to end. We had nowhere to go and no way of getting home to Australia, even if Jim could make it onto a plane, which was doubtful. He was a British citizen and the NHS was a respected medical system. It was just common sense.

Even so, Jim was becoming more and more belligerent in his refusal to go to hospital. It was completely irrational. I sat beside him, holding his hand, and told him how much I loved him. I told him gently about the smell that was coming from him. He said I was making it up. I told him that I was worried that he might die right here in front of me and the girls and that I wasn't going to let that happen. For the first time ever in our relationship, I spoke in direct defiance of Jim's wishes. I told him that, if he didn't come to the car with me now, I would call an ambulance to come and get him.

Jim was livid, but I could see in his face that he also felt helpless and it broke my heart to see my fearless knight in shining armour brought so low, knowing that my words had done it to him. He said he would go after he'd had a bath, and I stifled a sense of urgency. At least he had agreed to go. Standing in a shower was too much for him, so I ran a warm bath and helped him into it. Sitting was too painful for his back, so he sank into a kneeling position in the bath and leaned forward onto his hands. Frozen in that position, it was only a few seconds before Jim gasped at me to get him out. He looked like he was about to collapse face down into the water and I quickly pulled out the plug, before getting into the bathwater fully clothed to prop Jim up and help him out.

Shouldering as much of his weight as I could, we staggered back to the bed, soaking wet. Jim fell into bed moaning in pain and I quickly towelled him dry before covering him and throwing on some dry clothes myself. I ran downstairs to our B&B host, explained that Jim had collapsed and asked her to call an ambulance.

Back upstairs, I checked on Jim, who was lying where I'd left him, shivering and moaning in pain. I then went to the girls and told them that an ambulance would be coming to take Dad to hospital. Our amazing hosts had already offered to look after the girls so I could go with Jim to the hospital. Fear and worry were plain to see in their eyes and there was no way to fix it for them.

Did I want to leave my daughters with people who were virtually strangers to them? No! Was there another option? No. I needed to be with Jim, and the girls would not be allowed where he was going.

The paramedics arrived just as the first fat drops of rain began to fall from the pregnant clouds. They quickly assessed Jim and administered a vial of morphine. Jim's pain did not abate, so they gave him another and another and kept on until they reached the maximum dosage, but his pain remained strong. By the time they got Jim down the stairs on the trolley and into the ambulance, the rain had set in and was falling steadily. Our hosts assured us that the girls would be well looked after and that I should take all the time I needed. Kissing and hugging the girls goodbye, I jumped into the car and set off after the ambulance along the A40, following their lights and sirens through the gloominess of the day. It was my worst nightmare, another ambulance with lights and sirens. Not my son this time, now it was my husband.

The Oxford University Hospitals is a sprawling state-of-the-art medical complex. By the time I arrived, parked the car, went to reception and located Jim in his bed in the emergency department, the doctors had already seen him and run initial tests. Things were very different from our visit the previous week. Jim was sitting propped up in bed wearing a hospital gown with a drip in his arm. He was still in pain and the doctors had told him that there was a problem with his kidneys. Later we would learn that Jim's kidneys had shut down and he would have died within 24 hours if he hadn't gone to hospital. Because he had renal failure, the hospital was arranging to transfer him to another hospital with a specialist renal unit where he would commence dialysis.

The hospital housing the Oxford renal unit was very different from the schmick new university hospital. Built from brick on a single level in the 1940s, frankly it was old and tired. That didn't matter, though, because the quality of medical care was excellent. With the benefit of hindsight, I would say the quality of care was superior to Australia's insofar as it was more holistic and less profit-driven, more about what was best for the patient and less about what was best for the business.

The rain continued to fall relentlessly and it was getting dark. Jim was settled in and feeling more comfortable. We both agreed that I should go back to the girls as they would be wondering what was going on. I felt torn, not wanting to leave my love alone in hospital but knowing that our daughters needed the reassurance of my presence. I arrived back to find that our kind hosts had fed the girls dinner and they were happily ensconced in the lounge room, having been read the latest Harry Potter book, which was hot off the press and not yet available in Australia.

I hadn't eaten, but that was the least of my concerns. I told the girls that the doctors had worked out that Dad's kidneys were the problem and that he was already feeling better now that he was in hospital. I explained about the need for dialysis and told them that we would all go to visit him tomorrow.

Once the girls were tucked up in bed, I got on the phone and went to work. My first call was to the travel insurance hotline in Australia, updating them on Jim's medical details and commencing a claim. The accommodation in Paris and Loire Valley needed to be notified of our cancellation. We had to be out of our current accommodation but had nowhere to go. Our hosts had already offered me a single room for the three of us for the next couple of days, but that was all they could do. They were fully booked after that, so I needed to find us a place to stay – and fast.

Outside, the rain continued and I booked a room for one night in a hotel in Oxford, but they had nothing free for days after. The hotel receptionist had given me a list of hotels to call and I began working my way down the page. It was the same story each time. They were fully booked due the combination of peak holiday season and the floods in the west. Taking whatever I could get – a night here, two nights there – would mean packing up the girls and the car and moving around Oxford, but at least we would have a place to sleep and shower for the next few days while we waited to find out when Jim would be well enough to travel.

*It's Because I Love You*

www.ingramcontent.com/pod-product-compliance
Lightning Source LLC
Chambersburg PA
CBHW011149290426
44109CB00025B/2541